TEDDY KNITS

20 FABULOUS DESIGNS FOR SWEATERS, MITTENS, TOYS AND MORE

MELINDA COSS

AURUM PRESS

This book is dedicated to
Spencer Bear of Cambridge

First published 1989 by Aurum Press Limited
33 Museum Street, London WC1A 1LD

Produced by the Justin Knowles Publishing Group
9 Colleton Crescent, Exeter EX2 4BY

Design: Vic Giolitto
Photography: Jon Sturdy at Quicksilver
Models: Justine at Laraine Ashton and
Amanda Masters at Models 1
Make-up: Jan at A.J. Management

British Library Cataloguing in Publication Data

Coss, Melinda
  Teddy knits.
  1. Knitting. Pictorial designs
  I. Title
  746.43′2

  ISBN 1–85410–071–8

Typeset by Scribes, Exeter
Printed and bound in Italy by Amilcare Pizzi s.p.a.

CONTENTS

ABBREVIATIONS

alt	alternate(ly)
beg	begin(ning)
C6B	slip 3 sts onto a cable needle and hold at back, k3, k3 from cable needle
C6F	slip 3 sts onto a cable needle and hold at front, k3, k3 from cable needle
C8B	slip 4 sts onto a cable needle and hold at back, k4, k4 from cable needle
C8F	slip 4 sts onto a cable needle and hold at front, k4, k4 from cable needle
cm	centimetre(s)
cont	continue/continuing
dec	decrease/decreasing
inc	increase/increasing
k	knit
k1b	knit stitch through back loop

MB	make small bobble (*see* Techniques, page 9)
MBL	make large bobble
p	purl
psso	pass slipped stitch over
rep	repeat
RS	right side(s)
sl	slip
ssk	slip 1 stitch, knit 1 stitch, pass slipped stitch over
st(s)	stitch(es)
st st	stocking stitch
tbl	through back of loop(s)
tog	together
WS	wrong side(s)
yo	place yarn over right-hand needle from back to front to make another st
yrn	wrap yarn around right-hand needle from front to back to make another stitch

TECHNIQUES

READING THE GRAPHS

Throughout the book explanatory graphs show the colour designs charted out, with stitch symbols added where necessary. Each square represents one stitch across, i.e., horizontally, and one row up, i.e., vertically. The graphs should be used in conjunction with the written instructions, which will tell you where and when to incorporate them. Any colours required or symbols used will be explained in the pattern. Always assume that you are working in stocking stitch unless otherwise instructed.

If you are not experienced in the use of graphs, remember that when you look at the flat page you are simply looking at a graphic representation of the right side of your piece of work, i.e., the smooth side of stocking stitch. For this reason, wherever possible, the graphs begin with a right side (RS) row so that you can see exactly what is going on as you knit. Knit rows are worked from right to left and purl rows from left to right.

FAIRISLE

The technique of colour knitting called 'fairisle' is often confused with the traditional style of colour knitting that originated in the Fair Isles and took its name from those islands. Knitting instructions that call for the fairisle method do not necessarily produce a small-motifed repetitive pattern similar to that sported by the Prince of Wales in the Twenties — far from it, as can be seen from some of the patterns in this book.

The method referred to as fairisle knitting is when two colours are used across a row, with the one not in use being carried at the back of the work until it is next required. This is normally done by dropping one colour and picking up the other, using the right hand. If you are lucky enough to have mastered both the 'English' and 'Continental' methods of knitting, the yarns being used may be held simultaneously, one in the left hand, the other in the right hand. The instructions below, however, are limited to the more standard one-handed method and give the three alternative methods of dealing with the yarn not in use.

Stranding

Stranding is the term used to describe the technique by which the yarn not in use is simply left hanging at the back of the work until it is next needed. The yarn in use is then dropped and the carried yarn taken up, ready for use. This means that the strand, or 'float', thus produced on the wrong side of the work has a direct pull on the stitches either side of it.

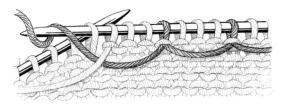

The wrong side of the work, showing stranding at the correct tension.

It is essential to leave a float long enough to span this gap without pulling the stitches out of shape and to allow the stitches in front of it to stretch and not to pucker on the right side of the work. It is preferable to go to the other extreme and leave a small loop at the back of the work rather than pull the float too tightly.

If the gap to be bridged by the float is wide, the strands produced may easily be caught and pulled when the garment is put on or taken off. This problem may be remedied by catching the floats down with a few stitches on the wrong side of the work at the finishing stage.

Weaving

With this method the yarn being carried is looped over or under the working yarn on every stitch, creating an up and down woven effect on the wrong side of the work. Since the knitter does not have to gauge the length of the floats, many people find that this is the easiest method of ensuring an even, accurate tension. Weaving does increase the chances of the carried colour showing through on to the right side of the

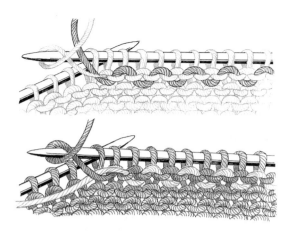

The wrong side of weaving, showing the up and down path of the carried yarn.

work, however, and it tends to produce a far denser fabric, which is not always desirable when a thick fibre is being used.

Stranding and weaving

Combining the two methods of stranding and weaving is invariably the most practical solution to the problem of working perfect fairisle. Most designs will have colour areas that will vary in the number of stitches. If the gap between areas of the same colour is only a few stitches, then stranding will suffice, but if the float produced will be too long, weave the carried yarn in every few stitches. Should you be unsure about the length of float to leave, slip your fingers under one. If you succeed with ease, the float is too long.

Stranding and weaving worked too tightly.

The most difficult aspect of fairisle knitting is getting the tension correct. This does not depend on the stitch size so much as on the way you treat the carried yarn. This is why, when working an all-over fairisle, you should always knit a tension sample in fairisle, not in main colour stocking stitch, as the weaving or stranding will greatly affect the finished measurement of the stitches. The most important rule to remember is that *the yarn being carried must be woven or stranded loosely enough to have the same degree of 'give' as the knitting itself.* Unless this is achieved, the resulting fabric will have no elasticity whatsoever and, in extreme examples, very tight floats will buckle the stitches so that they lie badly on the right side of the work.

If you are using the fairisle technique to work a colour motif on a single-colour background, keep the motif tension as close

If you are using the intarsia method, twist the yarns firmly together when you change colours.

to the background tension as possible. If there is a great difference, the motif stitches will distort the image.

INTARSIA

Intarsia is the term used for the technique of colour knitting whereby each area of colour is worked using a separate ball of yarn, rather than carrying yarns from one area to another as in the fairisle technique. Any design that involves large blocks of isolated colour that are not going to be repeated along a row or required again a few rows later, should be worked in this way.

There are no limitations to the number of colours that may be used on any one row other than those imposed by lack of patience and/or dexterity. Avoid getting into a tangle with too many separate balls of yarn hanging from the back of the work and remember that every time a new ball of yarn is introduced and broken off after use, two extra ends are produced that will have to be secured at the end of the day. When ends are left, always make sure that they are long enough to thread up so that they may be properly fastened with a pointed tapestry

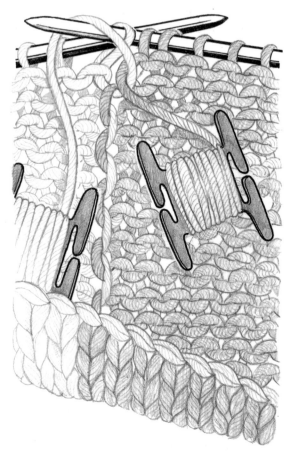

needle. Do this very carefully through the backs of the worked stitches to avoid distorting the design on the right side of the work. The ends that are left should never be knotted because they will make the wrong side of the work look extremely unsightly and they will invariably work themselves loose and create problems at a later stage.

If only a few large, regular areas of colour are being worked, avoid tangling the wool by laying the different balls of yarn on a table in front of you or keep them separate in individual jam jars or shoe-boxes. However, this requires careful turning at the end of every row so that the various strands do not become twisted.

The easiest method is to use small bobbins that hold each yarn separately and that hang at the back of the work. Such bobbins are available at most large yarn stores or they may be made at home out of stiff card. They come in a variety of shapes, but all have a narrow slit in them that keeps the wound yarn in place but allows the knitter to unwind a controlled amount as and when required. When winding yarn on to a bobbin, try to wind sufficient to complete an entire area of colour, but don't overwind, as heavy bobbins may pull stitches out of shape.

When you change colour from one stitch to another, it is essential that you twist the yarns around one another before dropping the old colour and working the first stitch in the new colour. This prevents a hole from forming. If it is not done, there is no strand to connect the last stitch worked in colour 'A' to the first stitch worked in colour 'B'. This twisting should also be done quite firmly to prevent a gap from appearing after the work has settled.

MAKING A BOBBLE

There are numerous variations on the theme of bobble making, but in this book we have used just two, which, for ease of identification, we have called large and small, abbreviated as MBL and MB. If worked on a right side (RS) row, the bobble will hang on the right side, if worked on a wrong side (WS) row, push it through on to the right side.

Large bobble

1. When the MBL position on the row has been reached, make 5 stitches out of the

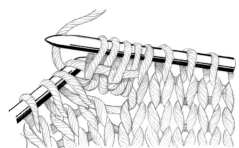
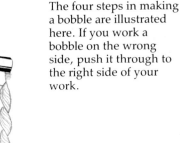

The four steps in making a bobble are illustrated here. If you work a bobble on the wrong side, push it through to the right side of your work.

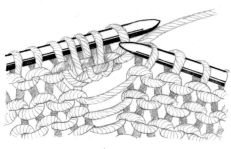

next one by knitting into its front, then its back, front, back and front again before slipping it off the LH needle.
2. Turn the work and knit these 5 stitches only.
3. Turn the work, purl 5 and repeat the last 2 rows.
4. Using the point of the left-hand needle, lift the bobble stitches, in order, over the first one on the right-hand needle, i.e., 2nd, 3rd, 4th and 5th, so that one stitch remains.

After completing the bobble, the work may continue as normal, the single stitch having been restored to its original position on the row.

Small bobble
To make a small bobble, as for the Rupert

9

design, k 3 sts from 1, turn, k3, turn, sl 1, k2 tog, psso.

CABLES

A basic cable is simply a twist in the knitted fabric caused by working a small number of stitches out of sequence every few rows. This is done by slipping the stitches on to a needle and leaving them at the front or the back of the work while the next stitches on the left-hand needle are worked. The held stitches are then worked normally. The cable, worked in stocking stitch, will always be flanked by a few reversed stocking stitches to give it definition. Since it does involve a twist, however, cabled fabric will always have a tighter tension than one worked in plain stocking stitch, so take extra care when working a tension sample.

Cable needles are very short and double-ended. Some have a little kink in them to help keep the stitches in place while others are being worked. Use one that is a similar size to the needles being used for the main work and take care not to stretch or twist the stitches when moving them from needle to needle.

On the right side of the work, if the stitches are held to the front, the cable will cross from the right to the left. If the stitches are held at the back of the work, the cable will twist from the left to the right.

Front cross cable
1. (RS): work to the six stitches that are to be cabled. Slip the next three stitches on the left-hand needle on to the cable needle and leave them hanging at the front of the work.
2. Knit the next three stitches on the left-hand needle as normal.
3. Knit the three held stitches off the cable needle.

Repeat this twist wherever indicated in the instructions.

The same basic technique may be used to move a single stitch across a background of stocking stitch at a diagonal, rather than form a cable that moves up the work vertically.

Where the abbreviation cb2 is used, the first stitch is slipped on to the cable needle and left at the back of the work while the next stitch is knitted. The held stitch is then knitted off the cable needle. Cf2 is the same but with the cable needle left at the front of

the work. On purl rows the abbreviations pcb2 and pcf2 are used to denote the same movement but in which the stitches are purled rather than knitted. In this way a continuous criss-cross line is formed.

SEAMS

After achieving the correct tension, the final sewing up of your knitting is the most important technique to master. It can make or break a garment, however carefully it may have been knitted. This is why the making up instructions after every set of knitting instructions should be followed exactly, especially to the type of seam to be used and the order in which the seams are to be worked.

Before starting any piece of work, always leave an end of yarn long enough to complete a substantial section, if not the whole length, of the eventual seam. After working a couple of rows, wind this up and pin it to the work to keep it out of the way. If required, also leave a sizable end when the work has been completed. This saves having to join in new ends that may well work loose, especially at stress points such as welts.

The secret of perfect-looking seams is uniformity and regularity of stitch. When

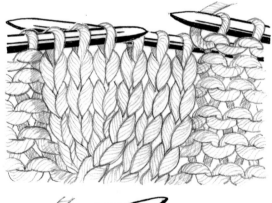

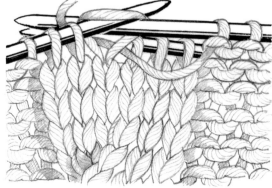

The front cross cable.

joining two pieces that have been worked in the same stitch, they should be joined row for row, and all work should be pinned first to ensure an even distribution of fabrics. When joining work that has a design on both pieces, take great care to match the colours, changing the colour you are using to sew the seam where necessary.

Backstitch

Pin the two pieces of work together, right sides facing, making sure that the edges are absolutely flush. Always leave as narrow a seam allowance as possible to reduce unnecessary bulk. It is essential that the line of backstitches is kept straight, using the lines of the knitted stitches as a guide. All the stitches should be identical in length, one starting immediately after the previous one has finished. On the side of the work facing you, the stitches should form a continuous, straight line. If the seam is starting at the very edge of the work, close the edges with an overstitch as shown. Now work the backstitch as follows:

1. Make a running stitch (maximum length 1cm), through both thicknesses of work.
2. Put the needle back into the work in exactly the same spot as before and make another running stitch twice as long.
3. Put the needle back into the work adjacent to the point where the previous stitch ended. Make another stitch the same length.

Keep repeating step 3 until the last stitch, which needs to be half as long to fill in the final gap left at the end of the seam.

By keeping the stitch line straight and by pulling the yarn fairly firmly after each stitch, no gaps should appear when the work is opened out and the seam pulled apart.

This seam is suitable for lightweight yarns or when an untidy selvedge has been worked.

Flat seam

This seam is a slight contradiction in terms since its working involves an oversewing action, but when the work is opened out it will do so completely and lie quite flat, unlike a backstitched seam.

Use a blunt-ended tapestry needle to avoid splitting the knitted stitches. Pin both pieces right sides together and hold the work as shown. The needle is placed through the

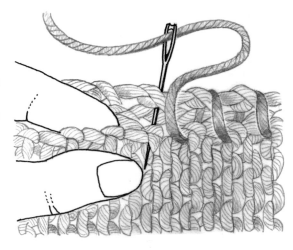

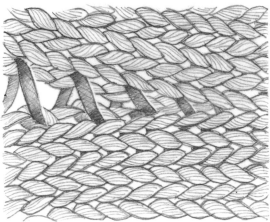

The drawings show (above) how you should hold the knitting to work a flat seam and (below) how your work will look on the right side.

very edge stitch on the back piece and then through the very edge stitch on the front piece. The yarn is pulled through and the action repeated, with the needle being placed through exactly the same part of each stitch every time. Always work through the edge stitch only. By taking in more than this, a lumpy, untidy seam that will never lie flat will be produced.

When two pieces of stocking stitch are to be joined with a flat seam, do not work any special selvedge such as knitting every edge stitch. Just work the edge stitches normally but as tightly as possible, using only the tip of your needle. When you come to work the seam, place the needle behind the knots of the edge stitches and not the looser strands that run between the knots, since these will not provide a firm enough base for the seam, which will appear gappy when opened out.

Flat seams are essential for heavy-weight yarns where a backstitch would create far too much bulk. They should also be used for attaching buttonbands, collars and so forth, where flatness and neatness are essential.

Borders, welts, cuffs and any other part of a garment where the edge of the seam will be visible should be joined with a flat seam, even if the remainder of the garment is to have a backstitched seam. Start with a flat seam until the rib/border is complete and then change over to a backstitch, taking in a tiny seam allowance at first and then smoothly widening it without making a sudden inroad into the work.

EMBROIDERY

To achieve the detail necessary for the facial features of some of the teddies incorporated into the garments, simple embroidery stitches have been added after the knitting has been completed. You may find it helpful to sketch roughly on to the fabric, using tailor's chalk or lines of very small pins, the position and outline of the embroidery.

Satin stitch
Satin stitch is used to 'in-fill' areas such as eyes. It is formed by working straight stitches, very close to one another, over the length of the area to be covered.

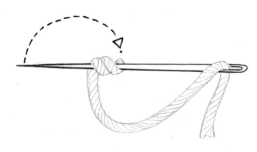

Backstitch
Outlines are worked in backstitch, which should be worked in exactly the same way as the stitch used for seams (*see* page 11). When you are working a curve, try to make very small stitches to ensure a continuous line.

Chain stitch
Bring needle up through back of work and back down at starting point and up again under loop. Pull through ready for the next stitch.

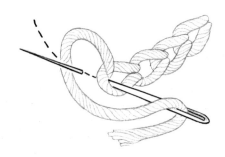

French knots
Push the needle through the knitting, wind wool twice around the needle, pull wool through and insert needle back at starting point.

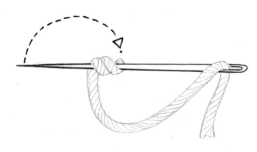

Daisy stitch
Bring needle up through back of work and back down at starting point and up again under and over loop. Bring needle up again at starting point and repeat chains in a circle to form a daisy.

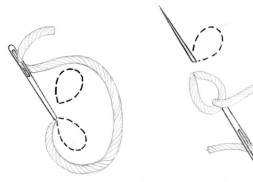

Keep the loops of chain stitch to the same tension and work in smooth curves.

French knots are used to make the centres of flowers.

When you embroider facial features such as eyes use satin stitch for solid areas and backstitch for outlines.

When you work daisy stitch, make sure that the loops are evenly sized and spaced.

Swiss darning

This is the most straightforward method of embroidery that may be worked on knitted fabrics since it exactly replicates knitted stitches. For this reason Swiss darning is sometimes called 'duplicate stitch'. By following the path of the knitted stitch with a contrasting colour, it is possible to create a variety of designs that have the appearance of being worked as a complicated fairisle, although they have, more simply, been added afterwards. For knitters who are not too confident with colour techniques, this is a very useful adjunct to their knitting skills.

When Swiss darning, always use a yarn of the same thickness as the knitting so that it will cover the stitch beneath it but not create an embossed effect. Use a blunt-ended tapestry needle to avoid splitting the knitted stitches as you embroider. The tension of the embroidered stitches must be kept exactly the same as the work that is providing the base so that they sit properly and do not pucker the work. The tension is regulated by how tightly the embroidery yarn is pulled through the work at each stage. Take great care when joining in and securing yarn ends on the wrong side of the work so that the stitches in the area do not become distorted.

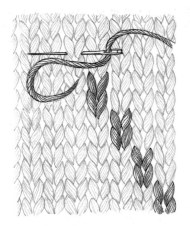

When you use Swiss darning to complete a motif, make sure that you use yarn of the same thickness as the knitting and that you follow the path of the knitted stitches.

MAKING A POMPON

Use a circular object measuring approximately 115mm across to draw and cut out two cardboard circles. Cut a smaller circle (approximately 25mm across) from the centre of each piece. Place these two circles together and wind your yarn through the centre hole and around the frame. Continue to wind the yarn evenly around the frame until the centre hole is almost full. Holding the circles firmly with your left hand, cut through all the yarn between the two edges of cardboard. Ease the two pieces of cardboard apart and firmly tie a length of yarn around the middle, leaving a loose end. Pull away the cardboard, gently fan out the yarn and trim. Attach the pompon to your garment by sewing the loose end to your garment.

BEAR ESSENTIALS

Materials
Wendy Miami – white: 250gm; red: 200gm; yellow: 100gm; green and turquoise: less than 50gm of each. Approximately 68cm of 2cm wide elastic. Scrap of black cotton for embroidery.

Needles
One pair of 3mm and one pair of 3¾mm needles; one 3mm circular needle.

Tension
Using 3¾mm needles and measured over st st, 20 sts and 28 rows = 10cm square.

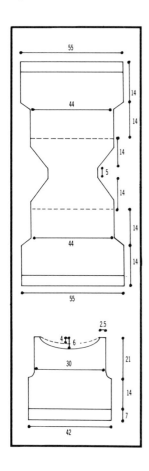

The graph opposite should be followed to complete the top (*see* pages 16–17).

This fun beach outfit is worked using the intarsia method (*see* Techniques, page 8). The pattern is worked to fit chest/hip sizes 81/91cm.

PANTS

Using 3¾mm needles and white, cast on 110 sts. Work in k2, p2 rib for 4 rows.

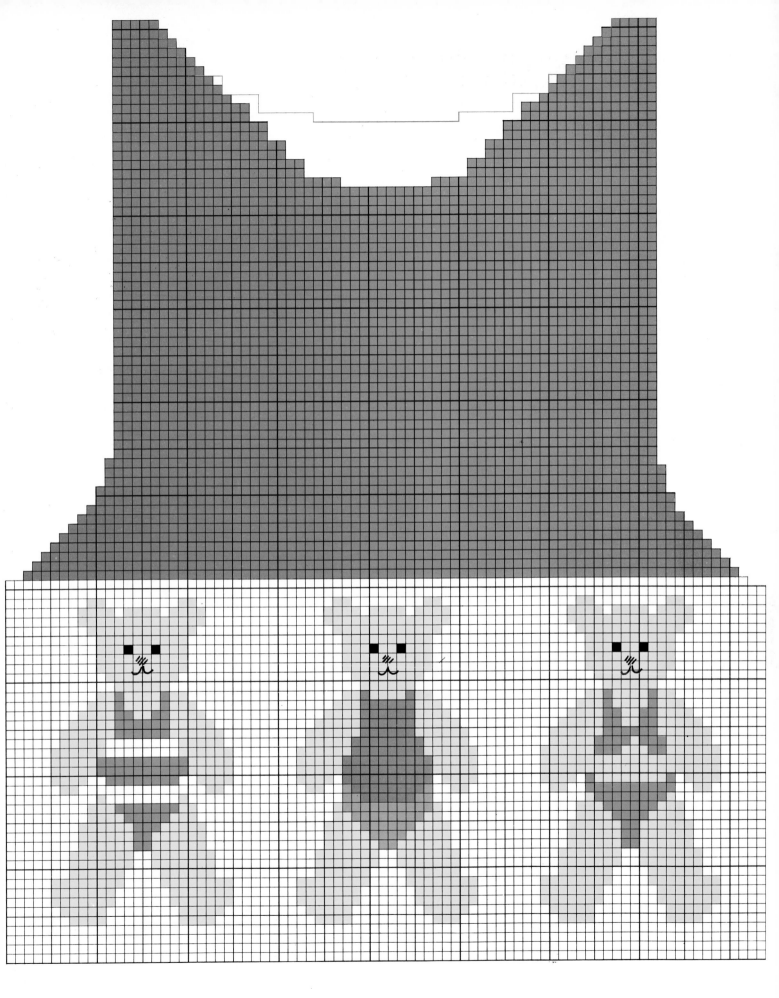

Incorporate this graph into the pants as described below.

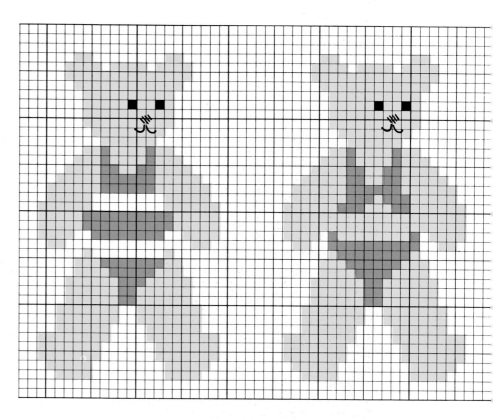

Commence working from the above graph in st st until it is complete.

Change to 3mm needles and red. Next row: k2, k2 tog, *k3, k2 tog,* rep from * to * to last st, k1 (88 sts). Work in k2, p2 rib for 14cm ending with a RS row.

Change to 3¾mm needles and white and, starting with a k row, work in st st for 10 rows. Dec 7 sts at beg of next 2 rows, 6 sts at beg of next 2 rows, 4 sts at beg of next 2 rows and 3 sts at beg of the following 2 rows. Dec 2 sts at beg of next 4 rows and 1 st at each end of the next 6 rows. Then dec 1 st at each end of the next 6 alt rows (16 sts). Work 9 rows without shaping. Dec 1 st at each end of the next row. Work 15 rows without shaping, inc 1 st at beg of the next row (16 sts). Inc 1 st at each end of the following 4th row, 1 st at each end of the 2 following 3rd rows, then the 12 following alt rows (46 sts). Cont by inc 1 st at each end of every row until you have 88 sts. Work 10 rows without shaping.

Change to 3mm needles and red and work in k2, p2 rib for 14cm.

Change to 3¾mm needles and white. K1, *inc into next st,* k3, inc into next st. Rep from * to * until 2 sts remain, k2. Turn the graph upside down and work until it is complete. K2, p2 rib for 4 rows. Cast off.

Making up

With RS together, join ribbed section with a flat seam and use a narrow backstitch on the skirt and pants. This will ensure that no seams show when the rib is folded.

Pants rib

With RS facing and using a 3mm circular needle, pick up and k 124 sts around leg edge. Work in k2, p2 rib for 3 rows. Cast off loosely ribwise.

TOP

Front

Using 3mm needles and red, cast on 84 sts. Work in k2, p2 rib for 7cm.

Change to 3¾mm needles and white and commence working from the graph on page 15 in st st until it is complete. Change to red.

Shape armhole: cast off 2 sts at beg of next 2 rows, then dec 1 st at each end of every row 8 times. Dec 1 st at each end of the next alt row and 1 st at each end of the following 3rd row*. Cont straight to neck shaping. Next row: k25, slip remaining sts onto a stitch holder and work on this side of the neck only. Keeping armhole edge straight, cast off 4 sts at beg of the next row, 2 sts at neck edge on the next 4 alt rows, then 1 st at neck edge on the next 8 rows. Work 1 row, cast off. Slip centre 10 sts onto a spare

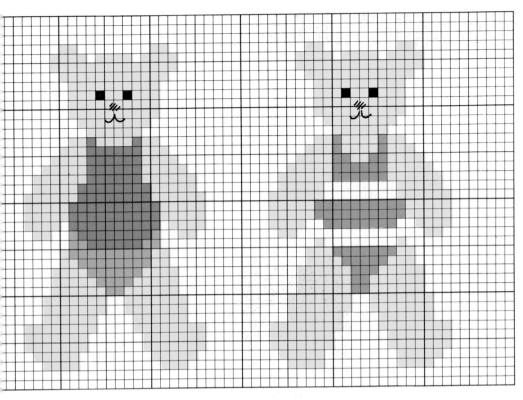

needle, rejoin yarn at neck edge and shape
second side of neck to match.

Back

Work as for front to *. Cont straight to back
neck shaping. K22, leave remaining sts on a
spare needle, work on this side of neck only.
Cast off 6 sts at beg of the next row, 4 sts at
beg of the next alt row and 3 sts at beg of the
next alt row. Cast off 2 sts at beg of the next
alt row, then 1 st at neck edge on the next
2 rows. Work 1 row. Cast off. Slip centre
16 sts onto a spare needle, rejoin yarn at
neck edge and shape second side to match.
Join shoulder seams.

Neckband

Using a 3mm circular needle and red, pick
up 100 sts evenly around the neck. Work in
k2, p2 rib for 3cm. Cast off.

Armhole ribs

Using a 3mm circular needle and red, pick
up 86 sts evenly around armhole. Work in
k2, p2 rib for 2cm. Cast off loosely ribwise.

Making up

Join side seams using a narrow backstitch.
Fold down skirt so that the red band is
folded in half, inserting elastic to fit. Sew
along bottom of red band through two
thicknesses. Embroider facial details.

17

LITTLE BEARS CARDIGAN

Materials
Wendy Family Choice
4-ply – forest (244) (A):
350gm; red (242) (B) and
gold (267): 50gm of each.
Wendy Ascot 4-ply –
autumn gold (412): 50gm.
8 small pearl buttons.

Needles
One pair of 2¾mm and
one pair of 3¼mm
needles.

Tension
Using 3¼mm needles and
measured over st st, 28 sts
and 28 rows = 10cm
square. Ribs worked on
2¾mm needles.

This Forties-style, crew-necked fitted
cardigan is worked using the fairisle method
(*see* Techniques, page 7).

Back
Using 2¾mm needles and A, cast on 122 sts.
Work in k1, p1 rib for 10cm, inc 16 sts evenly

BACK
18
31
49
10
44

SLEEVES
31
39
24
7
20

FRONT
14
5
13
31
10
21

Graph 2

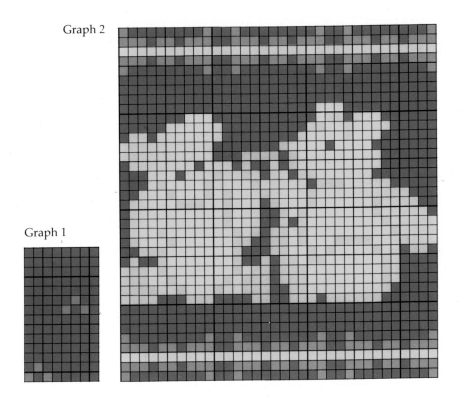

Graph 1

Graph 2 should be followed for the front and back of both the cardigan and the child's slipover, and for the sleeves of the cardigan.

Graph 1 should be incorporated into the front, back and sleeves of the cardigan as described on this page and on page 21, and into the front and back of the child's slipover, as described on pages 22–23.

across last row of rib (138 sts). Work 2 rows in st st in base colour only, commence working from graph 1, placing as follows: next row: k1(A), *k5(A), k1(B), k1(A), k1(B). Rep from * to last st, k1(A). Next row: p1(A), *p1(B), p6(A). Rep from * to last st, p1(A). Using A, work in st st for 5 rows. Next row: p1(A), *p4(A), p1(B), p1(A), p1(B), p1(A). Rep from * to last st, p1(A). Next row: k1(A), *k2(A), k1(B), k5(A). Rep from * to last st, k1(A). Using base colour only, work 5 rows in st st, then commence working from graph 2, positioning as follows: k1(A), work from graph repeating to last st, k1(A). Keeping the graph in this position, work until it is complete. Using base colour only, work in st st for 3 rows, return to graph 1 and work from this graph continuously (in position as previously set) until the back is complete. *At the same time*, when work measures 41cm from start, **shape armholes:** cast off 5 sts at beg of the next 2 rows, dec 1 st at each end of every row on the next 5 rows (118 sts). Cont working in pattern without further shaping until work measures 59cm. Leave sts on a spare needle.

Right front
Using 2¾mm needles and A, cast on 58 sts. Work in k1, p1 rib for 10cm, inc 10 sts evenly across last row of rib.
Change to 3¼mm needles and work 2 rows

of st st in A. Commence working from graph 1, placing as follows: row 1: k2(A), *k5(A), k1(B), k1(A), k1(B). Rep from * to the end of the row. Row 2: p1(A), p1(B), p6(A), rep from beg to last 2 sts, p2(A). Using A, work 5 rows in st st. Next row: p4(A), p1(B), p1(A), p1(B). Rep to last 2 sts, p2(A). Next row: k2(A), *k2(A), k1(B), k5(A), rep to end. Using A, work 5 rows in st st, then commence working from graph 2 which repeats exactly twice across the row. Work until the graph is complete. Using A, work 3 rows in st st. Return to graph 1 and work from this graph continuously (in position as previously set) until front is complete. *At the same time*, when work measures 41cm from the start (ending with a RS row), **shape armholes:** cast off 5 sts at beg of the next row, then dec 1 st at this edge on the next 5 rows (58 sts). Work 30 rows in pattern without further shaping. Next row (RS): **shape neck:** keeping in pattern, cast off 5 sts, work to end of row. Now dec 1 st at neck edge on every row until 38 sts remain. Work straight until front matches back. Leave sts on a spare needle.

Left front
Work as for right front reversing shapings.

Sleeves
Using 2¾mm needles and A, cast on 57 sts

and work in k1, p1 rib for 7cm, inc 11 sts evenly across last row of rib (68 sts). Change to 3¼mm needles and work 2 rows in st st, then commence working graphs in sequence and position as set for right front. *At the same time*, keeping in pattern (and working extra sts on graph 2 in A only), inc 1 st at each end of every 15th row until you have 87 sts. Work without further shaping until sleeve measures 46cm.

Shape sleeve head. Cast off 5 sts at beg of next 2 rows. Now dec 1 st at each end of every row until 65 sts remain. Dec 1 st at each end of every alt row until 33 sts remain. Cast off 4 sts at beg of the next 4 rows. Cast off remaining sts. Repeat for second sleeve.

Front bands

Using 2¾mm needles and A, cast on 10 sts and work in k1, p1 rib until the band fits from the bottom of the welt to the front edge of the neck when slightly stretched. Leave sts on a safety-pin. Place a pin to mark the first button position, 5 rows up from the cast-on edge. Mark 6 more button positions evenly up the band, making allowance for the 8th to be worked on the neckband. Work the buttonhole band to match the working buttonholes to correspond to marker pins. Work as follows: rib 4, cast off 2, rib 4. On the return row, cast on 2 sts over those cast off previously. When buttonhole band matches button band, leave sts on a safety-pin.

Neckband

Knit both shoulder seams tog, leaving back centre 45 sts on a spare needle. Using 2¾mm needles and A, rib the right-hand band sts on to the needle and, with RS of work facing, knit up 26 sts down right side of neck. K across back neck sts, then knit up 26 sts down left side of neck and rib the left-hand band sts (117 sts). Work in k1, p1 rib for 3 rows. Work buttonhole to correspond with others. Rib 2 more rows, cast off in rib.

Shoulder pads (Make 2)

Using 3¼mm needles and 2 strands of base colour yarn, cast on 2 sts. Work in garter st (knit every row) inc 1 st at each end of every row until you have 26 sts. Work without further shaping for 4cm. Cast off.

Making up

Pin bands to fronts and attach with a flat seam. Join side and sleeve seams with flat seams over the ribs and a narrow backstitch over the pattern. Set the sleeves in last, distributing the sleeve head evenly around the armhole. Attach buttons and shoulder pads.

LITTLE BEARS CHILD'S SLIPOVER

Materials
Wendy Family Choice 4-ply – red (242) (A): 200gm; forest (244) (B) and gold (267): 50gm of each; Wendy Ascot 4-ply – autumn gold (412): 50gm.

Needles
One pair of 2¾mm and one pair of 3¼mm needles.

Tension
Using 3¼mm needles and measured over st st, 28 sts and 28 rows = 10cm square. Ribs worked on 2¾mm needles.

The graphs for this pattern are on page 19.

A smart fairisle slipover to match mum's cardigan. The pattern is quoted in three sizes to fit children aged 4–5, 6–7 and 8–9 years.

Back
Using 2¾mm needles and A, cast on 83/97/111 sts.

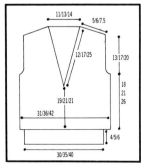

Row 1: k1, *p1, k1, rep from * to end.
Row 2: p1, *k1, p1, rep from * to end.
Rep these 2 rows until the work measures 4/5/6cm, inc 3/5/7 sts evenly across last row of rib (86/102/118 sts).
Change to 3¼mm needles and work 2 rows in st st starting with a knit row.
Next row: commence working from graph 2 as follows: size 1: k1 in A, knit from point on graph as indicated, rep complete graph to last stitch, k1 in A. Size 2: work from first stitch of graph, rep to end. Size 3: work from point on graph as indicated, rep to end. Work graph in this position until it is complete. Work three rows in st st in A only.
Next row (RS): commence working from graph 1, rep right across row. Cont following this graph until the back is complete. *At the same time*, when work measures 22/26/30cm, **shape armholes**: next row (RS): cast off 4 sts at beg of this and the next row, ** then dec 1 st at each end of every row until 68/80/96 sts remain. Work 1 row, then dec 1 st at each end of the next and every alt row until 60/70/82 sts remain. Work straight in pattern until back measures 35/43/52cm ending with a purl row.
Shape shoulders: cast off 7/9/11 sts at beg of the next 2 rows, then 7/8/10 sts at beg of the following 2 rows. Leave remaining 32/36/40 sts on a spare needle.

Front
Work as for back to **. Dec 1 st at each end of every row until 70/82/98 sts remain. Cont shaping armhole as for back and, *at the same time*, **shape neck**. Next row (RS): k2 tog, k31/37/45, k2 tog, turn and leave remaining sts on a spare needle. Cont on these 33/39/47 sts for the first side and work 1 row. Dec 1 st at each end of next and every alt row until 25/29/33 sts remain. Dec 1 st at neck edge only on every alt row until 17/26/31 sts remain, then on every following 3rd row until 14/17/21 sts remain. Work straight until front matches back to beg of shoulder shaping, ending with a WS row.
Shape shoulder: cast off 7/9/11 sts at beg of next row. Work 1 row, cast off remaining 7/8/10 sts.
With RS facing, join yarn to remaining sts. K2 tog, k to last 2 sts. K2 tog. Work to match first side, reversing shapings. Join right shoulder seam.

Neckband
Using 2¾mm needles, A and with RS facing, pick up and knit 39/49/63 sts down left side of neck, pick up loop at centre of 'V' and knit into back of it (mark this stitch with a coloured thread). Pick up and knit 39/49/63 sts up right side of neck, then k32/36/40 sts from back (111/135/167 sts).
Row 1 (WS): k1, *p1, k1, rep from * to within 2 sts of marked st. P2 tog, p1, p2 tog tbl, k1. **P1, k1, rep from ** to end.
Row 2: *p1, k1, rep from * to within 2 sts of marked st. P2 tog, k1, p2 tog tbl. **K1, p1, rep from ** to end. Rep these 2 rows twice more, then rep first row once more. Cast off evenly in rib, dec as before.
Join left shoulder seam and neck border.

Armbands
Using 2¾mm needles, A and with RS facing, pick up and knit 83/105/133 sts evenly around each armhole. Starting with a second row, work in rib as for back for 7 rows. Cast off evenly in rib.

Making up
Press work lightly on the wrong side. Join side seams using a flat seam. Join armband seams.

DANCING TEDDY MOHAIR LADIES' SWEATER

Materials
Wendy Soft Touch – blue
(67): 450gm; white (54):
100gm; sable (62): 50gm.
1m of 7mm wide satin
ribbon.

Needles
One pair of 4½mm and
one pair of 5½mm
needles.

Tension
Using 5½mm needles and
measured over st st, 16 sts
and 20 rows = 10cm
square.

This long-line fluffy sweater is covered in
dancing teddies.

Front
Using 4½mm needles and base colour, cast
on 86 sts. K1, p1 rib for 15cm inc 14 sts

evenly across last row of rib (100 sts).
Change to 5½mm needles cont following
graph to **neck shaping**: next row: k38, cast
off centre 24 sts, k38. Working on this last set
of sts only, dec 1 st at neck edge on every
row 7 times (31 sts). K4 rows in st st and

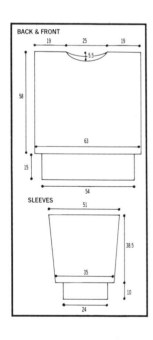

Follow the graph
opposite to complete the
front and the back of the
sweater; the dotted lines
indicate the areas to be
incorporated into the
sleeves (*see* page 27).

Graph 1

Graph 2

25

leave remaining sts on a spare needle. Rejoin yarn at inner edge and shape other side of neck to match. Leave shoulder sts on a spare needle.

Back

Work as for front to where shaping for back neck is indicated on graph. K33, leave centre 34 sts on a holder, k33. Working on this side of neck only, dec 1 st at neck edge on next 2 rows. Work 3 rows straight and leave remaining sts on a spare needle. Return to other side of neck, rejoin yarn at inner edge. Rep shaping leaving remaining shoulder sts on a spare needle.
With RS of back and front together, knit up the shoulder seams.

Right sleeve

Using 4½mm needles and base colour, cast on 38 sts. K1, p1 rib for 10cm, inc 18 sts evenly across last row of rib (56 sts). Change to 5½mm needles and, starting with a k row, work in st st, inc 1 st at each end of the 3rd row and the 12 following 6th rows (82 sts). *At the same time*, when 10 rows of st st have been worked, position graph as follows: k13, k first row of graph 2. K to end in base colour. Row 2: p13 in base colour,

p 2nd row of graph, p to end in base colour. Cont working graph in this position until it is complete. Cont shaping as set until you have 82 sts. Work 2 rows, cast off loosely.

Left sleeve

Work as for right sleeve but use graph 1 and do not place it until 36 rows of st st have been worked – i.e., row 37: k17 in base colour, k first row of graph 1, k17 in base colour. Row 38: p17, p 2nd row of graph 1, p17. Cont shaping as set until graph is complete and you have 82 sts on your needle. Work 2 rows. Cast off loosely.

Neckband

Using 4½mm needles and base colour, pick up 92 sts evenly around the neck. Work in k1, p1 rib for 10 rows, cast off loosely. Turn neckband inwards and slip st cast-off edge to pick-up edge.

Making up

Join sleeves to jumper, join side and sleeve seams using flat seams throughout. Embroider eyes, nose and mouth on teddies where indicated. Tie small bow of ribbon, catch into place under bear's chin.

GO EAT SOMEONE ELSE'S PORRIDGE

Materials
Wendy Ascot DK wool –
blue (937): 350gm; jade
(940): 200gm; black (423):
300gm; nut kernel (11),
chestnut (13), snowfall
(400), red poinsettia (426),
walnut (434) and crock of
gold (939), or colours to
match graph: less than
50gm of each.

Needles
One pair of 3¼mm and
one pair of 3¾mm
needles.

Tension
Using 3¾mm needles and
measured over st st, 24 sts
and 30 rows = 10cm
square. Ribs worked on
3¼mm needles.

A new slant to an old story – this oversized
jumper will fit both men and women. It is
worked in double-knitting wool using the
intarsia method (*see* Techniques, page 8).

The graph opposite
should be followed to
complete the front of the
jumper.

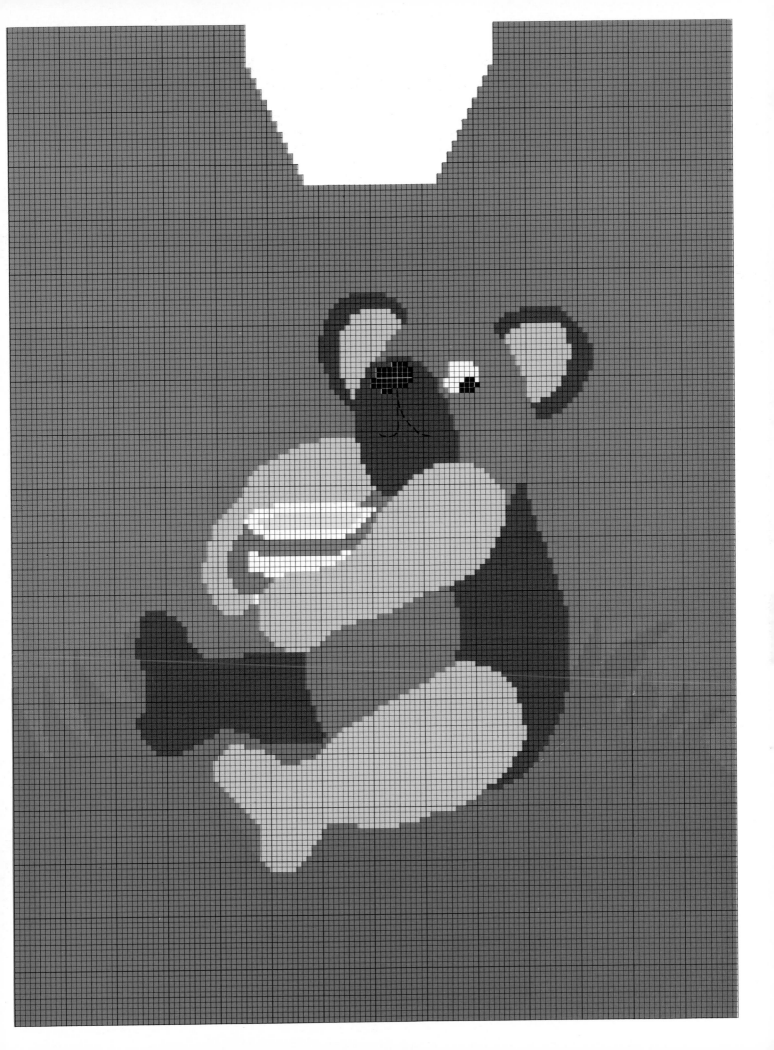

Incorporate this graph into the back of the jumper.

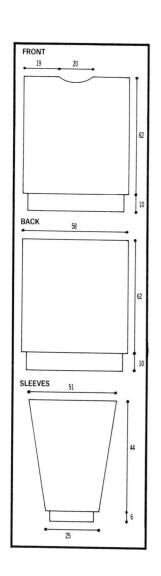

FRONT
19 20
62
10

BACK 58
62
10

SLEEVES 51
44
6
25

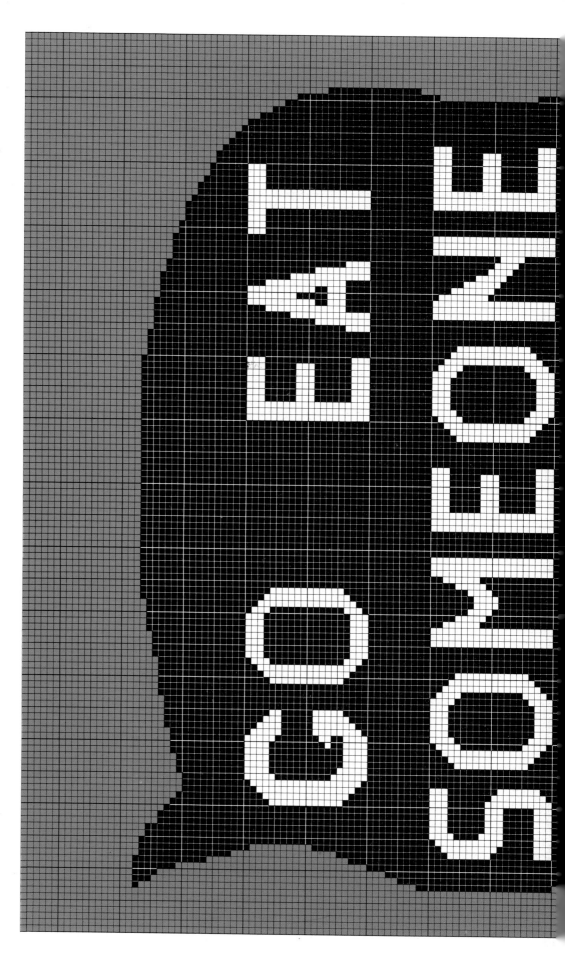

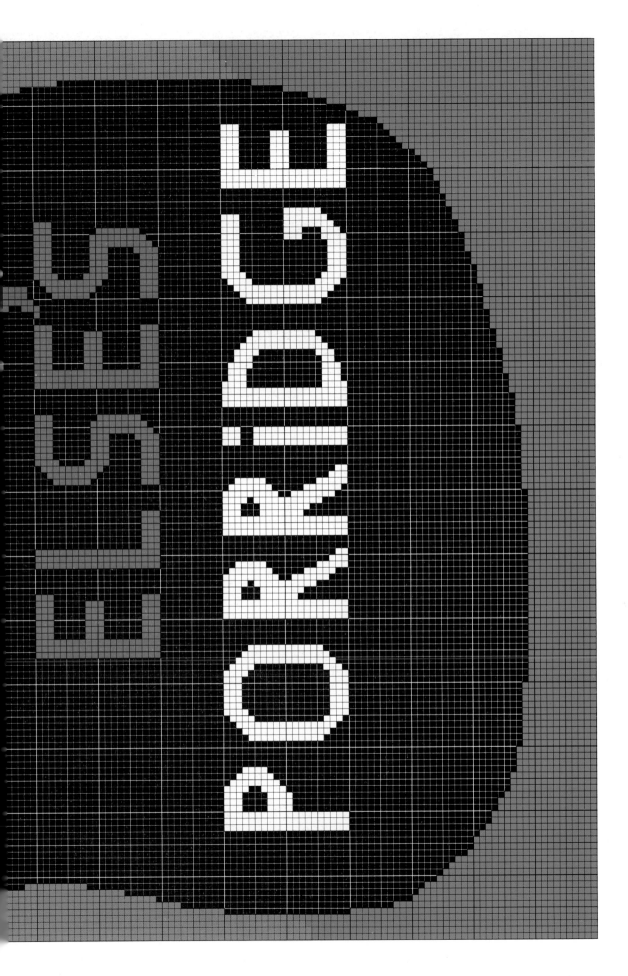

Front

Using 3¼mm needles and black, cast on 126 sts. Work in k1, p1 rib for 10cm, inc 14 sts evenly across last row of rib (140 sts). Change to 3¾mm needles and jade, commence following graph for front in st st to neck shaping. Next row (RS): k57, place these sts on a spare needle. Slip centre 26 sts onto a stitch holder, rejoin yarn, k57. Working on this last set of sts only, dec 1 st at neck edge on the next 11 alt rows. Work 8 rows without shaping, slip remaining 46 sts onto a spare needle. Rep for other side.

Back

Work as for front following graph for back (and ignoring neck shaping) until it is complete. Place a marker on the 46th st at each end for shoulder. Hold sts on a spare needle.

Sleeves

Using 3¼mm needles and black, cast on 56 sts and work in k1, p1 rib for 6cm. Inc 4 sts evenly across last row of rib (60 sts). Change to 3¾mm needles and cont in st st inc 1 st at each end of every 4th row until you have 124 sts. Work without further shaping until sleeve measures 50cm (including rib). Cast off loosely.

Neckband

Knit one shoulder seam together. Using 3¼mm needles and blue, pick up and knit the 48 sts held for centre back, 30 sts down one side of front, 26 sts held for centre front and 30 sts up other side of front (134 sts). Work in k1, p1 rib for 6cm. Cast off.

Making up

Knit second shoulder seam together. Turn neckband inwards and sl st cast-off edge to pick-up edge. Join sleeves to jumper, then join sleeve and body seams using a flat seam. Embroider mouth in black using backstitch.

Collar

Using 3¼mm needles, cast on 168 sts. Work in k1, p1 rib for 13cm, cast off. Sew collar to inside of neck (starting and ending at centre front).

USEFUL TEDDIES

Materials
Oddments of brightly coloured yarn in 4-ply or DK. A sheet of medium-weight card. A craft knife. Some rubber-based adhesive such as Copydex.

Needles
One pair of 3¼mm needles.

Tension
For once this doesn't matter, just take care to knit as evenly as possible.

Here are several ways to use up your odd scraps of yarn. In addition to these special graphs, the individual teddies from the Snowball Sleeping-bag (*see* page 61) have also been used.

TEDDY GREETINGS CARDS

Select the graph and colour of your choice and cast on the number of stitches required.

Work 2 rows of plain knitting in st st, then complete the graph. Work 2 more rows in base colour, then cast off. Steam press your completed work on the wrong side.
Place your square of knitting on the sheet of card and with a ruler, pencil a square around it to the size you would like your card to be, allowing at least 3cm all round. Cut the card to the same height as the square and three times the width (with the teddy in the middle). Fold the card inwards so that the right-hand edge meets the left side of the

The graphs opposite can be incorporated into greeting cards or even used to adorn a plain jumper.

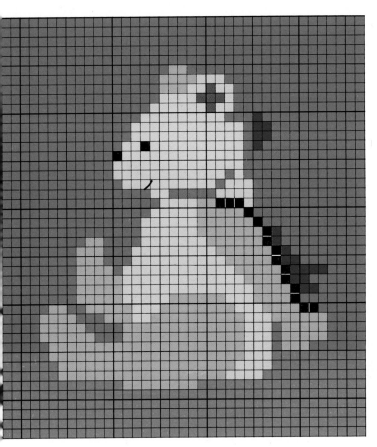

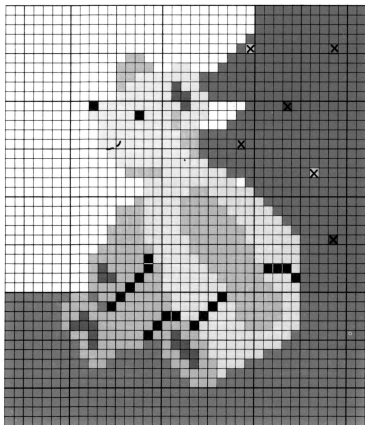

centre square. Then fold the left edge in to meet the right side of the centre square and make firm creases down both edges. Open the card up and, using the craft knife, cut a square to match the size of your knitting in between the two creases. Turn the card over and stick your teddy in the centre of one of the outer squares taking care to glue it evenly. Put more glue on the surrounding card and fold this back to the centre pressing it down firmly.

EMBROIDERED JUMPER

Brighten up a plain jumper by Swiss darning it with the motif of your choice. The jumper in the photograph was knitted to the basic squeaky pattern with the teddy embroidered with oddments of DK wool. For Swiss darning instructions, *see* Techniques, page 13.

EMBROIDERED CARDIGAN

Materials
Wendy Ascot DK wool –
ecru (401): 400gm. Wendy
Family Choice DK wool –
red (242), green (916),
yellow (267) and blue
(217): 50gm of each. A
scrap of black. 8 'ball-
shaped' buttons.

Needles
One pair of 4mm needles;
a medium-sized crochet
hook; a sharp darning-
needle.

Tension
Using 4mm needles and
measured over st st, 24 sts
and 30 rows = 10cm
square.

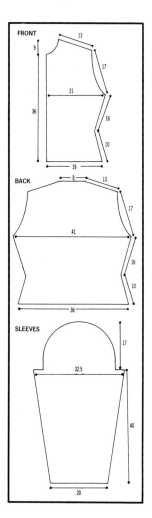

A Forties-style cable cardigan embroidered
with teddies and flowers, worked in double-
knitting wool.

Left front
Using 4mm needles and base colour, cast on
45 sts.

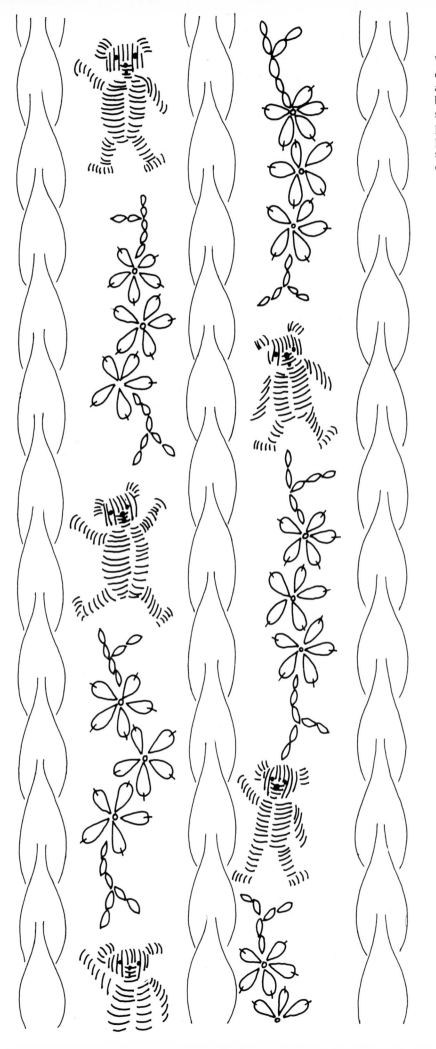

When you have completed the front, back and arms of the cardigan, but before you join the seams, embroider this pattern as described on page 40. The embroidery stitches needed are explained on page 12.

Row 1: k1, p21, k6, p8, k6, p2, k1.
Row 2: k3, p6, k8, p6, k22.
Rep these 2 rows twice.
Row 7: k1, p21, sl the next 3 sts onto a cable needle and hold at back of work, k3, k3 from cable needle (this will be described in future as C6R), p8, C6R, p2, k1.
Row 8: work as for row 2.
Row 9: k1, p12, k1, (p8, k6) twice, p2, k1.
Row 10: k3, (p6, k8) twice, p1, k13.
Row 11: k1, p11, k2, (p8, k6) twice, p2, k1.
Row 12: k3, (p6, k8) twice, p2, k12.
Row 13: k1, p10, k3, (p8, k6) twice, p2, k1.
Row 14: k3, (p6, k8) twice, p3, k11.
*Row 15: k1, p7, C6R, (p8, C6R) twice, p2, k1.
Row 16: k3, (p6, k8) 3 times.
Row 17: k1, p7, k6, (p8, k6) twice, p2, k1.
Row 18: work as for row 16.
Rep the last 2 rows twice more.*
The 8 rows from * to * form the pattern and are repeated throughout. Cont in pattern, inc 1 st at beg of the 4th cable row (counting from beg of the work on the cable rib nearest the front edge). Inc 1 st at the same edge on every following cable row until you have 51 sts. Cont in pattern without further shaping until 12 cable rows from the beg have been worked. Work 5 more rows of pattern (ending with a WS row). **N.B.** all extra sts should be purled – do not introduce another cable rib.
Shape armhole (RS): cast off 6 sts, p7, work in pattern to end. Cont in pattern, dec 1 st at beg of the next 3 alt rows (42 sts). Cont without further shaping until 16 cable rows from beg have been worked. Work 6 rows in pattern (ending at the neck edge).
Shape neck: cast off 7 sts at beg of the next row and, cont in pattern, dec 1 st at neck edge on the next and every following alt row until you have 32 sts. Cont in pattern without further shaping until 19 cable rows have been worked from beg. Work back to armhole edge. **Shape shoulder:** cast off 12 sts at beg of the next row and 10 sts at beg of the following 2 alt rows. Fasten off.

Right front
Using 4mm needles and base colour, cast on 45 sts.
Row 1: k1, p2, k6, p8, k6, p21, k1.
Row 2: k22, p6, k8, p6, k3.
Rep these 2 rows twice.
Row 7: k1, p2, slip the next 3 sts onto a cable needle and hold at front of work, k3, k3 from cable needle (this will be described in future

as C6L), p8, C6L, p21, k1.
Row 8: work as for row 2.
Row 9: k1, p2, (k6, p8) twice, k1, p12, k1.
Row 10: k13, p1, (k8, p6) twice, k3.
Row 11: k1, p2, (k6, p8) twice, k2, p11, k1.
Row 12: k12, p2, (k8, p6) twice, k3.
Row 13: k1, p2, (k6, p8) twice, k3 p10, k1.
Row 14: k11, p3, (k8, p6) twice, k3.
*Row 15: k1, p2, C6L, (p8, C6L) twice, p7, k1.
Row 16: (k8, p6) 3 times, k3.
Row 17: k1, p2, k6, (p8, k6) twice, p7, k1.
Row 18: Work as for row 16.
Rep the last 2 rows twice more.*
The last 8 rows from * to * form the pattern and are repeated throughout. From this point, work to match left front, increasing at the side edge at the end of the cable rows (instead of at the beg) and reading C6L instead of C6R. Reverse all other shapings.

Back
Using 4mm needles and base colour, cast on 86 sts.
Row 1: k1, p18, (k6, p8) 3 times, k6, p18, k1.
Row 2: k19, (p6, k8) 3 times, p6, k19.
Rep these 2 rows twice more.
Row 7: k1, p18, (C6R, p8) twice, C6L, p8, C6L, p18, k1.
Row 8: Work as for row 2.
Row 9: k1, p9, k1, (p8, k6) 4 times, p8, k1, p9, k1.
Row 10: k10, p1, (k8, p6) 4 times, k8, p1, k10.
Row 11: k1, p8, k2, (p8, k6) 4 times, p8, k2, p8, k1.
Row 12: k9, p2, (k8, p6) 4 times, k8, p2, k9.
Row 13: k1, p7, k3, (p8, k6) 4 times, p8, k3, p7, k1.
Row 14: k8, p3, (k8, p6) 4 times, k8, p3, k8.
*Row 15: k1, p4, (C6R, p8) 3 times, (C6L, p8) twice, C6L, p4, k1.
Row 16: k5, (p6, k8) 5 times, p6, k5.
Row 17: k1, p4, (k6, p8) 5 times, k6, p4, k1.
Row 18: Work as for row 16.
Rep the last 2 rows twice.*
The 8 rows from * to * form the pattern and are repeated throughout.
Cont in pattern, inc 1 st at each end of the 4th cable row (counting cable rows from beg of the work on the centre cable) and cont to inc 1 st at each end of every following cable row until you have 98 sts. **N.B.** All extra sts should be purled – do not start a new cable. Cont in pattern without further shaping until 12 cable rows from the beg have been worked. Work 5 rows in pattern.

Shape armholes: cast off 4 sts at beg of the next 2 rows, then dec 1 st at each end of the next row and every following alt row until 86 sts remain. Cont without further shaping until 19 cable rows have been worked from the beg. Pattern 1 row. **Shape shoulders**: cast off 12 sts at beg of the next 2 rows. Cast off 10 sts at beg of the next 4 rows. Cast off remaining 20 sts.

Sleeves (Both alike)
Using 4mm needles and base colour, cast on 48 sts.
Row 1: k1, p13, k6, p8, k6, p13, k1.
Row 2: k14, p6, k8, p6, k14.
Rep these 2 rows twice.
Row 7: k1, p13, C6R, p8, C6L, p13, k1.
Row 8: work as for row 2.
These 8 rows form the pattern and are repeated throughout. Cont in pattern, inc 1 st at each end of the next and every following 6th row until you have 78 sts (purling all extra sts). Cont in pattern without further shaping until 15 cable rows have been worked from the beg. Pattern 1 row.
Shape top: next row (RS): cast off 8 sts at beg of the next 2 rows, then dec 1 st at each end of the next and every following alt row until 48 sts remain. Cont without further shaping until 20 cable rows have been worked from the beg. Pattern 1 row. Cont as follows.
Row 1: k2 tog, p10, p2 tog, k6, p2 tog, p4, p2 tog, k6, p2 tog, p10, k2 tog.
Row 2: k2 tog, k10, p6, k6, p6, k10, k2 tog.
Row 3: k2 tog, p7, p2 tog, k6, p2 tog, p2, p2 tog, k6, p2 tog, p7, k2 tog.

Row 4: k2 tog, k7, p6, k4, p6, k7, k2 tog.
Row 5: k2 tog, p4, p2 tog, k6, p2 tog twice, k6, p2 tog, p4, k2 tog.
Row 6: k2 tog, k4, p6, k2, p6, k4, k2 tog.
Row 7: k2 tog, p1, p2 tog, C6R, p2 tog, C6L, p2 tog, p1, k2 tog.
Row 8: k2 tog, k1, p6, k1, p6, k1, k2 tog.
Cast off.

Embroidery
Press all pieces lightly on the wrong side. Following the embroidery chart, work the teddies in yellow using satin stitch. Work the daisies in daisy stitch using red and blue and making yellow French knots in the centre. Using green wool, work the flower stems in green chain stitch (all the embroidery stitches are described in Techniques, *see* page 12). The teddies' eyes and noses are worked using a small single stitch in black wool.

Making up
Using flat seams throughout, join side and sleeve seams and set in the sleeves.

Crochet edge and buttonholes
With RS of work facing and using a medium-sized crochet hook, start at the bottom right front and with blue wool make a single chain of crochet up the right front, around the neck and down the left front. Evenly space eight pins up the left front to mark positions for buttons. Using red wool, make a second chain of crochet up the right front working 4 chain sts instead of a single stitch opposite the button markers. Press lightly.
Stitch on the buttons.

SPENCER BEAR AND SON

A pair of cuddly bears that are worked in a choice of yarns using fur stitch. Papa bear is 54cm tall when seated, while his son stands approximately 34cm tall.

Stitches (Fur stitch)

Row 1 (RS): k1, *k1, but do not drop stitch off left-hand needle, bring yarn forward between needles and wind over left thumb to form a loop. Take yarn between needles to back and k the same stitch again, dropping it off the left-hand needle. Bring yarn forward between needles and take it over right-hand needle to make a loop, pass the 2 sts just worked over this loop and off right-hand needle. K next st,* rep from * to *.
Row 2: knit.
Row 3: k2, rep from * to *.
Row 4: knit.

Body

Using 4mm needles, cast on 22/44 sts. K 1/2 rows. Next row: k, inc into every st (44/88 sts). Rep these 2 rows once more (88/176 sts).

Materials
Wendy Dolce brown (100) or Merino DK camel (236) – **large bear** 1000gm; **small bear** 300gm. One pair of amber glass eyes. Terylene stuffing. Oddment of black wool.

Needles
One pair of 4mm needles.

Tension
Using 4mm needles and measured over st st, 24 sts and 32 rows = 10cm square.

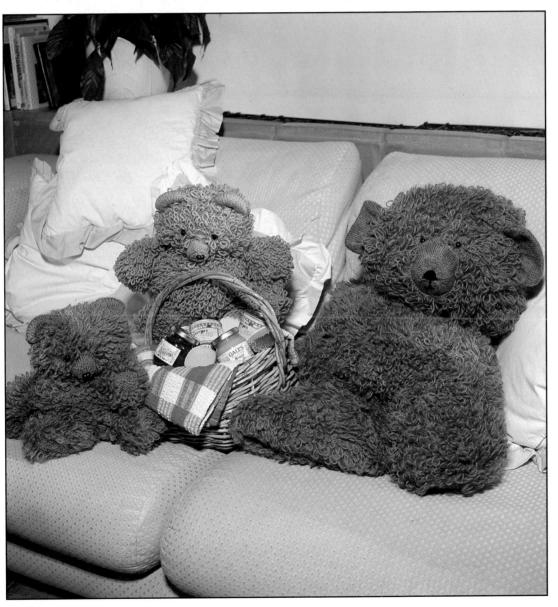

Commence working in fur st, starting at row 1 * for 27/54 rows. Next row: (k2 tog, k18, k2 tog) 4/8 times (80/160 sts). K 1/2 rows. Next row: (k2 tog, k16, k2 tog) 4/8 times (72/144 sts). Still working in fur st, work 15/30 rows straight. Next row: **k2 tog, rep from ** to end (36/72 sts). K 2/4 rows. Next row: k2 tog right across row (18/36 sts). Work 2/4 rows. Cast off.

Head
Work as for body to *. Work in fur st for 21/42 rows, then work as for body until you have 72/144 sts. Work 11/22 rows. Cont by shaping as for body until you have 18/36 sts, then cast off.

Legs (Make 2)
Starting at the foot, cast on 44/88 sts. K 1/2 rows. Next row: k17/34, (inc into next st)

When you come to make up the bear, sew the seams in the order given on page 43.

10/20 times. K17/34 (54/108 sts). K 1/2 rows. Next row: k22/44, (inc into next st) 10/20 times, k22/44 (64/128 sts). Begin working in fur st from row 1 and work 7/14 rows. Cont working in fur st. Next row: k22/44, (k2 tog) 10/20 times, k22/44, (54/108 sts). K 1/2 rows. Next row: k17, (k2 tog) 10/20 times, k17 (44/88 sts). Work 17/34 rows straight in fur st. Cast off loosely.

Arms (Make 2)

Start at shoulder, cast on 8/16 sts. K 1/2 rows. Begin working in fur st from row 1, inc 1 st at each end of every row until you have 44/88 sts. Work in fur st for 16/32 rows straight. Next row: k2 tog, right across row 22/44 sts. K 1/2 rows. Rep the last 2 rows once (11/22 sts). Next row: k1, (k2 tog) 5/10 times (6/12 sts). Break off yarn, thread it through the remaining sts, draw up tight and fasten off.

Nose

Cast on 32/64 sts. Work 4/8 rows in st st. Next row: (k2 tog, k6) 4/8 times (28/56 sts). Next row: (k5, k2 tog) 4/8 times (24/48 sts). Next row: (k2 tog, k4) 4/8 times (20/40 sts). Next row: (k3, k2 tog) 4/8 times (16/32 sts). Next row: (k2 tog, k2) 4/8 times (12/24 sts).

Next row: (k1, k2 tog) 4/8 times (8/16 sts). Break off yarn and thread it back through the remaining sts. Draw up tight and fasten off.

Ears (Make 2)

Cast on 18/32 sts and work in st st for 6/12 rows. Dec 1 st at each end of the next 2/4 rows. Work 1/2 rows, inc 1 st at each end of the next 2/4 rows. Work in st st for 6/12 rows. Cast off.

Making up

Sew all seams invisibly working on the wrong side. Fold head in half and join centre back seam. Stuff firmly. Fold nose in half and join seam. Sew to head, stuffing as you go. With black wool, embroider nose over centre seam. Attach eyes to head either side of top of nose. Join head seam. Join and stuff body. Stitch head firmly to body by oversewing. Fold ears in half and stitch short ends together. Stuff lightly and sew along bottom seam and gather slightly, sew to head. Fold arms in half and sew up sleeves leaving a 5cm opening at the narrow end. Stuff and stitch to body. Fold legs in half and join seam which is at the centre back, stuff and stitch firmly to body in sitting position.

TEDDY BOOTEES

Materials
Wendy Peter Pan DK yarn
– spring-lamb (868) and
lemon (803): less than
50gm of each. ½m of 1cm
wide satin ribbon. Scrap
of brown wool for
embroidery.

Needles
One set of 4 double-
pointed 3¾mm needles.

Tension
Using 3¾mm needles and
measured over st st, 24 sts
and 30 rows = 10cm
square.

A pretty pair of teddy bootees to keep baby's
toes snug.

Bootees
Using 3¾mm double-pointed needles and

white, cast on 10 sts. Work in garter stitch for 38 rows. Join in yellow, p 1 row. Next row: k twice into every stitch (20 sts). Next row: p12, turn, k4, turn, p3, turn, k2, turn, p3, turn, k4, turn, p5, turn, k2 tog, k1, k2 tog, k to end. Work 3 rows in st st. Next row: *k4, k2 tog, rep from * to end. Next row: *p3, p2 tog, rep from * across row. Next row: *k2, k2 tog, rep from * across row. Next row: k2 tog across row, then p2 tog across row to last st, p1. Next row: k2 tog, k1, k2 tog. Next row: sl 1, p2 tog, psso, fasten off.

Change to white and, starting halfway across cast-on edge with RS facing, pick up and knit 5 sts across heel, 18 sts across side edge, 10 sts across last row of white (under teddy's head), 18 sts down second edge, 5 sts across heel. Work 5 rounds in st st, then **shape toe:** k31, ssk, turn (leaving remaining 23 sts unworked). Next row: k7, k2 tog, turn, k7, ssk, turn. Next row: k7, ssk, turn. Rep the last 2 rows 6 times more, turn, work to end. Next row: *k1, yo, k2 tog, rep from * to end. K 1 round, cast off knitwise.

Making up

Embroider a knot in brown on the end of teddy's snout, with a small vertical and horizontal line beneath for his nose. Make two knots for eyes. Turn teddy's head back onto bootee toe and join by stitching around face (leaving ears free). Thread a length of satin ribbon through eyelets at top of bootee and tie in a bow.

BEARS AND BEES

Materials
Wendy Aran Tweed –
crofter (590): 550gm.
Wendy Soft Touch – sable
(62): 50gm. Wendy Aran
– antelope (516): 50gm.
Wendy Action Knit – blue
(513): 100gm; black (530):
50gm. Wendy Family
Choice DK (used double)
– yellow (267): 50gm.

Needles
One pair of 4mm and one
pair of 5mm needles; one
4mm circular needle.

Tension
Using 5mm needles and
measured over st st, 18 sts
and 22 rows = 10cm
square. Ribs worked on
4mm needles.

This boxy, tweedy aran-weight jumper is
worked using both the intarsia and fairisle
methods (*see* pages 7–8).

Front
Using 4mm needles and base colour, cast on
96 sts. Work in k1, p1 rib for 6cm.

Follow the graph
opposite to complete the
front and back of the
jumper. The dotted line
around the honey-pot
graph indicates the area
of the pocket that should
be knitted into the front.
The bear graph should be
incorporated into the
right sleeve and the two
bee graphs into the left
sleeve as described on
page 49.

46

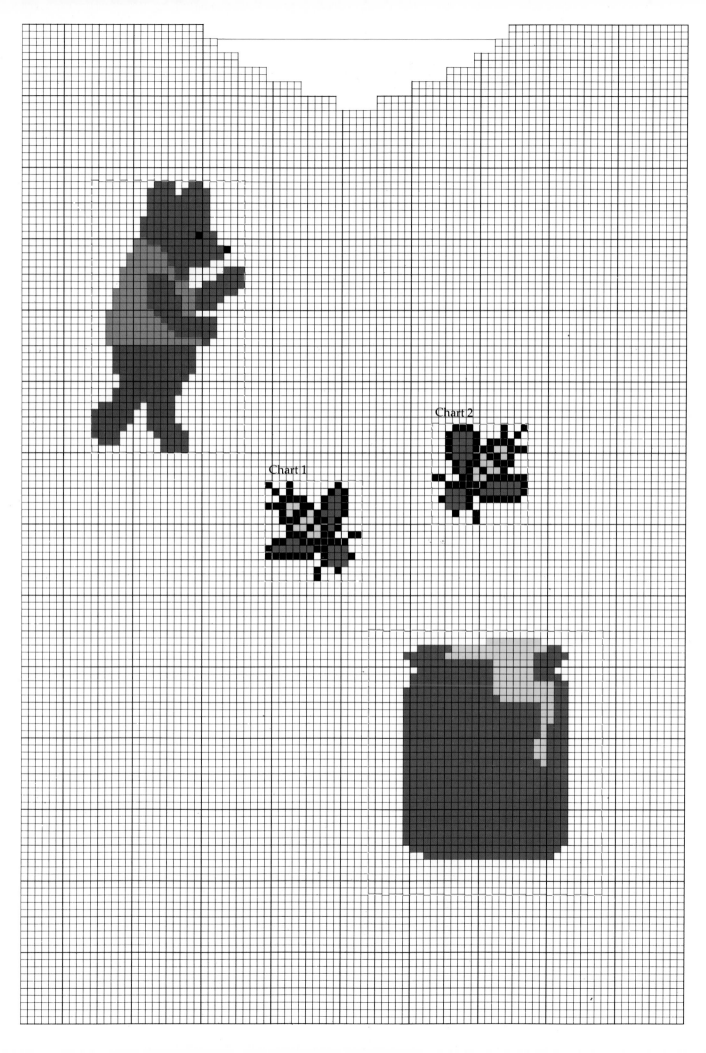

Chart 1

Chart 2

Change to 5mm needles and commence following graph in st st for 18 rows. **Pocket opening**: next row: k46, slip the last 34 sts from the right-hand needle onto a stitch holder, k to end. Next row: p50, turn, cast on 34 sts, turn, p to end. Cont following graph working new sts in base colour only. Work straight to neck shaping. Next row (RS): k45, cast off 6, k45. Working on the last set of sts only, *p back to neck edge, turn, cast off 5 sts, k to end, rep from * once more. P back to neck edge, turn, cast off 4 sts, k to end. Cast off 3 sts at neck edge on the next alt row and 2 sts at neck edge on the following alt row. Work 1 row, cast off loosely. Rejoin yarn at neck edge on remaining sts and shape to match first side. **Pocket**: pick up the 34 sts held for pocket and work the honey-pot graph until it is complete. Work 1 row. Change to 4mm needles, k1, p1 rib for 3 rows. Cast off. Stitch pocket into position.

Back

Work as for front but do not work pocket, simply knit honey-pot motif into main body of jumper in position as shown. Cont following the graph to back neck shaping. Next row (RS): k70 sts, slip the last 44 sts worked off the right-hand needle onto a stitch holder, k to end. Turn, p26, turn, cast off loosely. Rejoin yarn to other side of neck at inner edge. Work 1 row, cast off loosely.

Right sleeve

Using 4mm needles and base colour, cast on 50 sts. Work in k1, p1 rib for 6cm. Change to 5mm needles* and work 3 rows in st st, inc 1 st at each end of the next row.

Work 2 rows in st st. Commence working from bear graph positioning as follows: k15, k across the 22 sts of the graph, k15. Complete the graph, inc 1 st at each end of the next row and every following 4th row until you have 100 sts. Work 3 rows, then cast off.

Left sleeve

Work as for right sleeve to *. Cont in st st inc 1 st at each end of every 4th row until you have 100 sts. *At the same time*, when you have just completed your increase to 82 sts, work first bee graph, positioning thus: k42, k the 14 sts of graph, k26. Working shaping as set, complete this graph and cont until you have just worked your increase to 92 sts. Next row (RS): k27, k the 14 sts of the second bee graph, k51. Cont shaping as set and complete graph in position. When you have completed your shaping to 100 sts, work 3 rows and cast off.

Neckband

Sew both shoulder seams together and, using a 4mm circular needle, pick up and k 168 sts evenly around the neck. Work in k1, p1 rib for 4cm. Cast off loosely in rib. Slip st cast-off edge to pick-up edge. **Collar**: using 4mm needles and base colour, cast on 124 sts. Work in k1, p1 rib for 13cm. Cast off. Sew cast-off edge of collar to inside seam of neckband, leaving a centre front opening.

Making up

Join sleeves to jumper using a narrow backstitch. Join side and sleeve seams using flat seams.

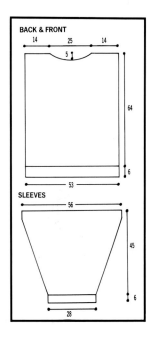

LITTLE BEARS

Materials
For two white and two brown teddies: Wendy Soft Touch – white (54) and sable (62): 50gm. Wendy Family Choice Chunky – oddments in assorted colours. Scraps of black DK wool for eyes and noses and a small quantity of terylene stuffing. **Pram toy** 1m of corded elastic; 11 wooden beads. **Mobile** 2×36cm and 4×14cm lengths of stiff wire and some nylon thread.

Needles
One pair of 4mm needles.

Tension
Using 4mm needles and measured over st st, 20 sts and 20 rows = 10cm square to produce a teddy 13cm tall.

These little mohair bears are quick to knit and make ideal gifts at Christmas time. String them together and you have a delightful pram toy, or make your own nursery mobile.

TEDDY

(Half body)

Beginning at legs, cast on 10 sts in mohair and work 18 rows in st st. **Shape arms**: k4, cast off 1 st, slip last stitch back onto the left-hand needle, cast on 18 sts and k to end. Work 4 rows in st st. Next row: p5, cast off 18 sts. P4, break yarn, slide stitches to end of needle. Work another half body in the same way but do not break yarn.

Head

RS: k across the remaining 18 sts, p 1 row. Next row: k10, turn, p4, turn, k3, turn, p2, turn, k3, turn, p4, turn, k2 tog twice, k to end. Work 3 rows in st st. Next row: *k4, k2 tog, rep once from *, k4. Next row: p. Next row: k3, k2 tog, rep once, k4. Next row: p. Next row: k2, k2 tog, rep to last 2 sts, k2. Break yarn and thread it back through loops, pull up tightly and secure.

Making up

Sew up centre back, front and arm seams of body, leaving a small hole in back for stuffing. Stuff body and head. Using a small piece of black wool, make a knot for teddy's nose on the end of his snout. Make a small vertical and horizontal stitch below the nose for his mouth. Make two knots for the eyes.

Ears

Pick up 3 sts from the side of teddy's head, inc once into each st (6 sts). Work 2 rows,

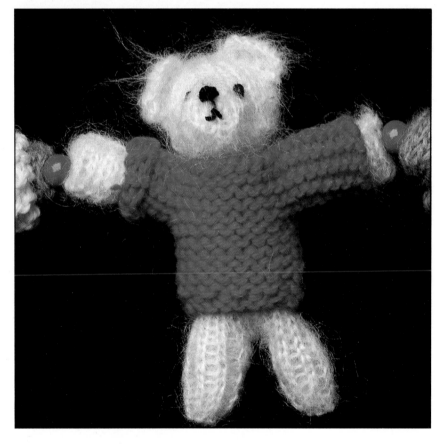

then cast off. Rep for other side. Stitch sides
of ears to head.

JUMPER

Using 4mm needles and bright chunky wool,
cast on 11 sts. Work 1 row in k1, p1 rib. K 12
rows. Cast on 7 sts at beg of the next 2 rows.
K 8 rows. Next row: k8, cast off 9, k8. Next
row: k8, cast on 9, k8. K 7 rows. Cast off 7
sts at beg of the next 2 rows, k 12 rows.
Work 1 row in k1, p1 rib, then cast off.

Making up
Place jumper over teddy's head, sew up
underarm and side seams.

PRAM TOY

Using a blunt needle, thread the elastic
through 4 beads, one bear, one bead, one
bear, one bead, one bear, one bead, one
bear, four beads. Form a loop of elastic at
each end and knot, threading the waste
elastic back through the end beads.

MOBILE

Take the two longer lengths of wire and
make small loops at each end. Cross the two
wires in the middle and close firmly with a
pair of pliers. Hang four lengths of nylon
thread off the loops and attach the shorter
lengths of wire (with loops at each end). Tie
lengths of nylon to the centre head of eight
teddies and hang them at each end of the
shorter lengths of wire.

THE BEAR'N~STEINS

A contemporary pair of bears with a love for traditional knitwear.

MR & MRS BEAR'N-STEIN

Right leg
Using 3¾mm needles, cast on 32 sts. Work in st st for 8 rows.*
Next row: k9, k2 tog, k7, k2 tog, k12.
Next row: p12, p2 tog, p5, p2 tog, p9.
Next row: k9, k2 tog, k3, k2 tog, k12.
Next row: p12, p2 tog, p1, p2 tog, p9 (23 sts).

Work 26 rows in st st, leave sts on a spare needle.

Left leg
Work as for right leg to *.
Next row: k12, k2 tog, k7, k2 tog, k9.
Next row: p9, p2 tog, p5, p2 tog, p12.
Next row: k12, k2 tog, k3, k2 tog, k9.
Next row: p9, p2 tog, p1, p2 tog, p12.
Work 26 rows in st st. K across sts for both legs on next row (46 sts). Work 36 rows in st st for body. **Shape shoulders:** next row: k8. Cast off 10 sts. K10, cast off 10 sts. K8.

Materials
Wendy Ascot DK wool – **male teddy** thatch (403): 150gm; **female teddy** hazelnut (411): 150gm. **Fairisle sweater** ecru (1) (A) – plum (408) (B), hazelnut (411) and black (423): 50gm of each. **Female's guernsey** Wendy Family Choice Aran – cream (524): 50gm. **Skirt** Ascot DK wool – red (426): 50gm. **Male's trousers** Ascot DK wool – lovat (437): 50gm. Small button. Small bag terylene stuffing.

Needles
One pair of 3¾mm and one pair of 4mm needles. One set of double-ended 3¼mm needles. One cable needle.

Tension
Using 3¾mm needles and measured over st st, 24 sts and 32 rows = 10cm square. This tension produces a bear approximately 35cm tall.

Follow this graph when you make the fairisle jumper.

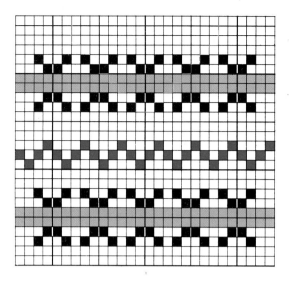

The dotted line around the muzzle indicates the line of the gathering thread.

Head

Ignoring the cast-off shoulders, p twice into every stitch (52 sts) – i.e., the shoulders will form 2 loops which will eventually be seamed at the top. Work in st st for 4 rows.
Shape muzzle: k20, k2 tog, k8, sl 1, k1, psso, k20.
Next row and every alt row: purl.
Row 3: k20, k2 tog, k6, sl 1, k1, psso, k20.
Row 5: k20, k2 tog, k4, sl 1, k1, psso, k20.
Row 7: k20, k2 tog, k2, sl 1, k1, psso, k20 (44 sts).
Work 6 rows in st st.
Next row (WS): p18, p2 tog 13 times (31 sts).
Work 9 rows in st st.
Next row: k2 tog 15 times, k1 (16 sts).
Next row: p2 tog 8 times (8 sts). Slip sts off needle and break yarn. Thread yarn back through sts and gather up tightly.

Ears (Make 2)

Cast on 14 sts, work 10 rows in st st, then cast off.

Arms

Using 3¾mm needles, cast on 16 sts. Working in st st, inc 1 st at each end of every row 3 times (22 sts). Work 4 rows straight, then dec 1 st at each end of every row 3 times (16 sts). Work 13 rows straight, then **shape top:** dec 1 st at each end of every row 4 times. Cast off remaining 8 sts. Rep for second arm.

Making up

Working all seams on the inside of your work, fold legs and feet in half lengthwise and sew up inside leg seams. Stuff legs and feet firmly. Join back and back head seam, stuffing as you go. Add extra stuffing to muzzle, making sure that it protrudes. Then, working with length of base colour yarn and starting at the neck, thread the yarn around the muzzle and gather it up (*see* diagram). Embroider eyes by oversewing in black, in position as shown. Sew a triangle for the nose and oversew in black. Embroider mouth and stitch from nose down to mouth using three large stitches (*see* diagram). Fold ears in half, with the longest edges together, and stitch along the bottom, gather slightly along this edge and sew into position as indicated. Sew up arm seams to where top shaping begins and stuff. Stitch arm-tops neatly onto body so that the centre arm-top touches the centre shoulder. Stitch across shoulders.

FAIRISLE JUMPER

Front

Using 3¾mm needles and base colour, cast on 28 sts.
Row 1: k1A, *p2B, k2A, rep from * to last st, k1A.
Row 2: p1A, *k2B, p2B, rep from * to last st, p1A.
Rep these last 2 rows once more, then commence following graph in st st to neck shaping.
Next row (RS): work pattern for 13 sts, turn, dec 1 st, p to end. Working on this side of the neck only, dec 1 st at neck edge on the next 6 rows (6 sts). Work 3 rows. Cast off. Rejoin yarn at neck edge, cast off 2 sts, work to end. Cast off 1 st at neck edge on next 7 rows. Work 2 rows. Cast off.

Back
Work as for front ignoring neck shaping. Work to shoulder line, cast off.

Sleeves (Both alike)
Work as for front until the row of zig-zags has been completed. Work 3 rows in base colour only, cast off.

Neckband
Join shoulder seams. With a set of 4 double-ended 3¼mm needles and with RS of work facing, start at the bottom of the V-neck and pick up 48 sts evenly around neck. Work back and forth in k1, p1 rib and base colour only for 3 rows. Cast off in plum.

TROUSERS

Using 3¾mm needles and a contrast colour, cast on 30 sts.
Row 1 (RS): *p2, k1, rep from * to end.
Row 2: *p1, k2, rep from * to end. Rep these 2 rows until work measures 14cm. Work 5 rows in st st. Cast off. Make the second leg in the same way.

Making up
Sew in all ends on the fairisle jumper. Sew sleeves to body. Join side and sleeve seams. Lay trouser legs side by side. Fold each leg in half lengthwise. Join legs together at centre front and back from the st st waistband downwards for 4cm to form the crutch. Join inside leg seams. Sew small button centre front on trouser waistband. Fold up trouser bottoms to form turn-ups.

ARAN JUMPER

Front
Using 4mm needles and ecru aran-weight wool, cast on 34 sts. Work 4 rows in k1, p1 rib. Cont in pattern as follows:
Row 1: k4, slip next 3 sts onto a cable needle and hold at front of work. K3, k3 from cable needle, k6, p2, k6, slip 3 sts onto a cable needle and hold at back of work. K3, k3 from cable needle, k4.
Row 2: p15, k4, p15.
Row 3: k14, p6, k14.
Row 4: p13, k8, p13.
Row 5: k4, slip next 3 sts onto a cable needle, hold at front of work, k3, k3 from cable needle, k2, p10, k2, slip next 3 sts onto a cable needle and hold at back of work, k3, k3 from cable needle, k4.
Row 6: p12, k10, p12.
Row 7: k13, p8, k13.
Row 8: p14, k6, p14.
Row 9: k4, slip next 3 sts onto a cable needle and hold at front of work, k3, k3 from cable needle, k5, p4, k5, slip next 3 sts onto a cable needle and hold at back, k3, k3 from cable needle, k4.
Row 10: p16, k1, k4 from next stitch, pass first 3 sts over 4th stitch to make bobble, p16. These 10 rows make your pattern. Rep them twice more. K 1 row. Next row: p8, k18, p8. Next row: cast off 8 sts. K18, k8. Next row, cast off 8 sts. K18, turn, cast off remaining 18 sts.

Back
Work exactly as for front.

Sleeves (Make 2)
Using 4mm needles, cast on 34 sts. K1, p1 rib for 4 rows, then work in knit only until sleeve measures 8cm. Cast off.

Making up
Join shoulder seams. Join sleeves to jumper, join side and sleeve seams.

SKIRT

Using 4mm needles and DK wool, cast on 66 sts. K 2 rows, then work in st st, starting with a knit row until skirt measures 13cm, ending with a p row. Next row: *k1, k2 tog, rep from * to end, k1. Work 4 rows in k1, p1 rib. Cast off. Join side seam.

RUPERT SWEATER

Materials
Wendy Ascot DK wool –
blue (425): 550gm; yellow
(6): 100gm; black (423):
100gm; white (400): 50gm;
red (426): 50gm. 3 buttons
2cm in diameter.

Needles
One pair of 3¼mm and
one pair of 4mm needles.
One cable needle.

Tension
Using 4mm needles and
worked over st st, 24 sts
and 32 rows = 10cm
square. Ribs worked on
3¼mm needles.

Rupert Bear has been a firm family favourite for generations. Our designer sweater, worked in cable and moss stitch diamonds, is strictly for the more experienced knitter.

Back

Using 3¼mm needles, cast on 111 sts and work in k1, p1 rib (row 1: k1, *p1, k1, rep from * to end. Row 2: p1, *k1, p1, rep from * to end). Rep these 2 rows until work measures 8cm, inc 27 sts evenly across last row (138 sts).

Change to 4mm needles and work from chart with cables at sides setting sts as follows:

Row 1: sl 1, p2, k8, p2, k8, p2, graph 92 sts, p2, k8, p2, k8, p2, k1 tbl.

Row 2: sl 1, k2, p8, k2, p8, k2, graph 92 sts, k2, p8, k2, p8, k2, k1 tbl.

Using sts thus set, cont to work cables on 9th and then every following 8th rows on side panels as follows:

Row 9: sl 1, k2, C8F, p2, C8F, p2, graph 92 sts, p2, C8B, p2, C8B, p2, k1 tbl.

Work rows 1–130 from graph, then rep rows 2–68 (total of 197 rows).

Shape shoulders: next row (RS): cast off 12 sts at beg of the next 6 rows, then cast off 13 sts at beg of the next 2 rows, leave remaining sts on a holder for collar.

Front

Work as for back until row 130 from graph has been completed. Now rep from row 2 again, but this time working centre diamond (Rupert motif) all in moss stitch. Cont until row 14 has been completed.

Front opening: work 65 sts from graph and turn, work on these sts for first side, cont from chart for a further 31 rows.

Neck shaping: next row (WS): cast off 4 sts, work to end, dec 1 st at neck edge on next 12 rows, then cont until work measures same as back to shoulder.

Shape shoulder: next row (RS): cast off 12 sts at beg of the next and 2 following alt rows, work 1 row, cast off remaining sts. Rejoin yarn to remaining sts, cast off 8 sts at centre front, work on remaining sts to match first side, reversing all shapings.

Sleeves

Using 3¼mm needles, cast on 50 sts and work in k1, p1 rib for 8cm, inc 10 sts evenly across last row (60 sts).

Change to 4mm needles and work from graph, starting at Row 5, and inc 1 st at each end of every third row as indicated, when there are 92 sts on needle. Cont from graph, inc at each end of every 3rd row as before until you have 126 sts. Cont working inc sts in moss stitch as set. After last inc, cont until row 120 has been completed. Cast off all sts.

Buttonband

Join shoulder seams. Using 3¼mm needles and with RS of work facing, pick up and knit approximately 24 sts down left front neck opening. Work in k1, p1 rib until band fits neatly across centre front (8 sts). Cast off ribwise.

Mark position for 3 buttons on centre row of this band, the first to come on 3rd st from centre front, the last to come on 3rd st from neck edge and the other spaced evenly between.

Buttonhole band

Work as for buttonband, working buttonholes opposite marked positions as follows.

Buttonhole row

At each marked position, k2 tog, yrn.

Collar

Using 3¼mm needles and with RS of work facing, starting just off centre (towards neck) of buttonhole band, pick up and knit 3 sts from band, 4 cast-off neck sts, approximately 20 sts up right front neck, back neck 40 sts, approximately 20 sts down left front neck, 4 cast-off neck sts and 3 sts from button-band. Work in k1, p1 rib for 8cm. Cast off loosely ribwise.

Making up

Set sleeves into place, the centre of sleeve to shoulder seam and set the rest evenly at each side. Sew into place. Sew button and buttonhole band at centre front cast-off sts, with the buttonband underneath. Sew side and sleeve seams. Sew on buttons to match buttonholes. Embroider scarf as indicated on photograph, using backstitch.

The graph overleaf (on pages 58-9) should be followed to complete the front and the back of the sweater and also the sleeves. The key for the graph is given below, and for instructions on making a bobble (see page 9). The black lines on Rupert's scarf should be embroidered, using backstitch, when the sweater is complete.

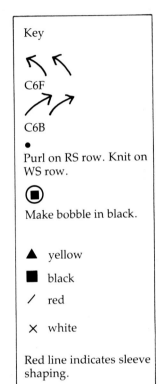

Key

C6F

C6B

• Purl on RS row. Knit on WS row.

⬤ Make bobble in black.

▲ yellow

■ black

／ red

✕ white

Red line indicates sleeve shaping.

58

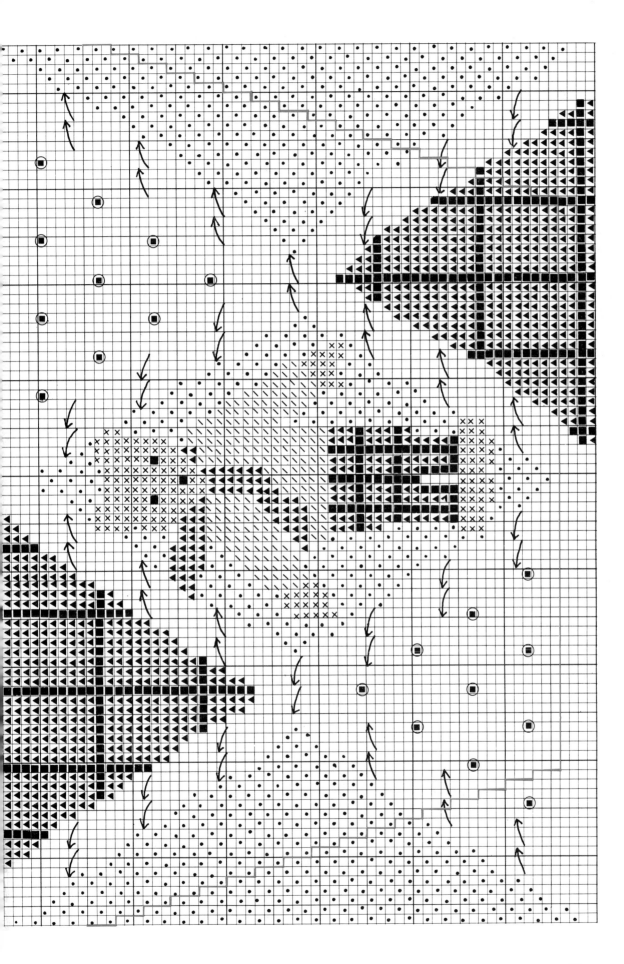

SNOWBALL SLEEPING-BAG

Snug as a teddy in a rug, this woolly sleeping-bag is worked in a cable check with motifs using the intarsia method (*see* Techniques, page 8).

Materials
Wendy Family Choice DK yarn – red (242): 250gm; colours to match the graph, purity (212), Côte d'Azur (216), Sahara (202), black (247), amber fire (267), neon flash (903) and emerald isle (205): less than 50gm of each. A 31cm nylon zip.

Needles
One pair of 3½mm and one pair of 4mm needles; one cable needle.

Tension
Using 4mm needles and measured over st st, 22 sts and 32 rows = 10cm square.

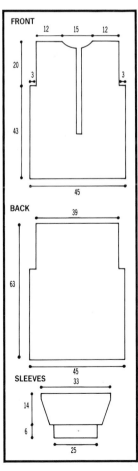

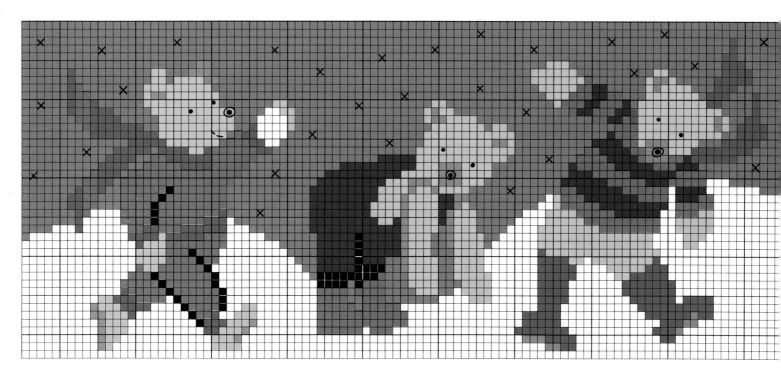

Incorporate the top graph into both the front and the back of the sleeping-bag. The crosses indicate where bobbles should be made in white (*see* page 9), and the dots indicate where the bears' noses should be completed, in black, by knitting three from one stitch and passing the first two stitches over the fourth loop.

The lower graph should be followed to complete the sleeves (*see* page 64). The crosses indicate where bobbles should be worked in white (*see* page 9).

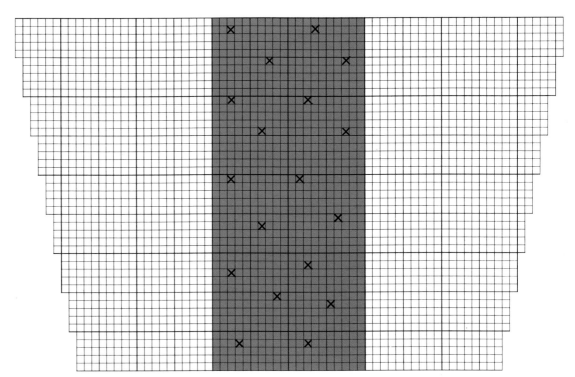

Pattern: Cable check
Rows 1, 3, 5 and 7: k12, p12.
Row 2 and alt rows: k the p sts and p the k sts of the previous row.
Row 9: cross 2R (slip 2 sts onto a cable needle and hold at back of work, k next 2 sts, then k the 2 sts from cable needle), k4, cross 2L (slip 2 sts onto a cable needle and hold at front of work, k next 2 sts, then k the 2 sts from cable needle), p12.
Rows 11, 13, 15 and 17: work as row 1.

Rows 19, 21, 23 and 25: p12, k12.
Row 27: p12, cross 2R, k4, cross 2L.
Rows 29, 31, 33 and 35: work as row 19.
Row 37: rep from row 1.

Front
Using 4mm needles and base colour, cast on 100 sts. Commence working in pattern, placing as follows:
Row 1: k2, rep row 1 of pattern 4 times across the row, k2.

Row 2: p2, rep row 2 of pattern 4 times across the row, p2.

Cont in pattern and work in st st the 2 extra sts at either end of the row until 36 rows have been worked.

Next row (RS): working in st st only (and making bobbles for noses and snowflakes as indicated on the graph), commence following graph until it is complete (take care to use separate balls of yarn for each colour – i.e., do not use the fairisle technique). When the graph is complete, change back to base colour and p 1 row.

Make zip opening: commence working in pattern from row 1: starting with k2, rep pattern twice. Leave remaining 50 sts on a spare needle and cont working in pattern on this first set of 50 sts only. When 56 rows have been worked, **shape armholes:** next row (RS): cast off 7 sts at beg of this row and cont working in pattern for another 40 rows. Next row (WS): **shape neck:** cast off 7 sts at beg of the next row, dec 2 sts at neck edge on the next 2 alt rows and 1 st at neck edge on the next 6 alt rows. Work 6 rows, then cast off. Rejoin yarn at neck edge to sts held for other side and work to match, reversing shapings.

Back

Work as for front until the graph is complete. Cont straight in pattern until back matches front to armhole shaping, then cast off 7 sts at beg of next 2 rows. Work straight until back matches front to shoulder. Cast off.

Sleeves

Using 3½mm needles and base colour, cast on 42 sts. Work in k1, p1 rib for 6cm, inc 14 sts evenly across last row of rib (56 sts). Commence following graph working base colour in moss st – i.e., row 1: k1, p1. On row 2 p the k sts and k the p sts of the previous row. Work the blue centre panel in st st making bobbles where indicated on the graph. *At the same time*, inc 1 st at each end of every 5th row until you have 72 sts. Work 5 rows straight, cast off. Make second sleeve to match.

Making up

Join one shoulder. Using 3½mm needles and base colour, pick up and k 75 sts evenly around the neck, beginning at the RS neck edge. K1, p1 rib for 5 rows, cast off. Join sleeves to body, join sleeve and side seams using flat seams throughout. Carefully stitch a 31cm zip into place.

TEDDY LEGWARMERS, HAT AND MITTENS

A bright collection of hat, mittens and legwarmers in a teddy and jacquard pattern worked using the fairisle method (*see* Techniques page 7).

Materials
Wendy Family Choice DK wool – green (271): 200gm; ecru (230), yellow (267), rose (269) and black (247): less than 50gm of each.

Needles
One pair of 3¼mm and one pair of 4mm needles. One pair of 3¼mm and one pair of 4mm double-ended needles.

Tension
Using 4mm needles and measured over st st, 24 sts and 32 rows = 10cm square.

Incorporate the graphs into the legwarmers, mittens and hat as described. Work one teddy only for the mittens.

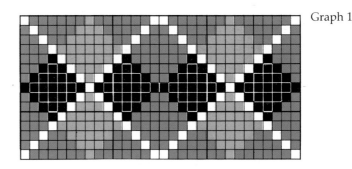

Graph 1

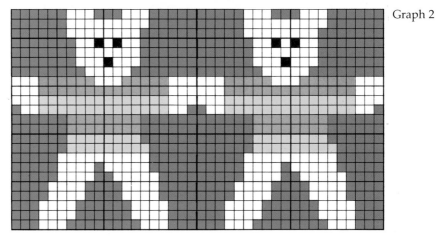

Graph 2

LEGWARMERS

Legs (Both alike)

Using 3¼mm needles and green (base colour), cast on 60 sts. Work in k2, p2 rib for 30 rows, inc 1 st at each end of the last row. Change to 4mm needles and work 2 rows in st st. *Commence following graph 2, working as follows: k1 in base, work 3 repeats from graph, k1 in base. Cont as set until graph is complete. Work 3 rows in base colour only, then follow graph 1 as follows: work 1 st in base, work 4 repeats from graph across row, k1 in base. Work 3 rows in base colour only,* repeat from * to *.
Change to 3¼mm needles, and, dec 1 st at each end of the first row, work 14 rows in double rib. Cast off loosely. Join side seams.

MITTENS

Using 4mm needles and base colour, cast on 36 sts. Work 4 rows in st st. Commence working from graph 1, placing as follows: k3, k first row of graph, k3. Cont working in graph as set until it is complete. Work 3 rows in base colour only.
Change to 3¼mm needles and work 23 rows in k1, p1 rib inc 7 sts evenly across last row of rib.

Next row (WS): change to 4mm needles and, commencing with a knit row, work in st st for 22 rows. **Divide for thumb:** next row: k 3 sts, place the next 6 sts on a safety-pin, cast on 6 sts, k to end. Work 2 rows in base colour only. Commence working from graph 2 until it is complete. Cont in base colour only until mitten measures 15cm from last row of rib, ending with a WS row. **Shape top:** next row: k1, sl 1, k1, psso, k to last 3 sts, k2 tog, k1. Next row: p. Rep these 2 rows until 33 sts remain. Cast off.
Complete thumb: using 4mm double-pointed needles and with RS of work facing, k across 6 sts on safety-pin, k up 1 st, then k up 6 sts across cast-on sts of palm (13 sts). Cont in rounds of st st for 5cm. **Shape top:** next row: k2 tog to last st, k1 (7 sts). Cut yarn, thread through remaining sts, pull up and fasten off.
Make second mitten to match, reversing shapings.

Making up
Sew up side seam. Fold cuff back to right side.

TEDDY HAT

Using 3¼mm double-pointed needles and
base colour, cast on 134 sts. Work in k1, p1
rib for 4cm, inc 16 sts evenly across last row
of rib (150 sts). Change to 4mm double-
pointed needles and work 2 rounds in base
colour only. Commence following graph 1
and work until complete. Work 3 rounds in
base colour only, then work from graph 2 as

follows. Work 7 teddies across row, then
work 13 sts in base colour only and complete
graph as set. Work 3 rounds in base colour
only, rep graph 1. Cont straight in base
colour only until hat measures 23cm. Next
row: k2 tog, rep across row. Break yarn and
thread it back through the remaining 75 sts.
Pull up tightly and secure. Make a pompon
(*see* Techniques page 13) in base colour and
attach to top of hat.

PADDINGTON BEAR'S DUFFLE COAT

Materials
Wendy Ascot Chunky –
red (426): 350/350/350/
1,000gm; black: 50/50/50/
100gm; blue (398), yellow
(399), dark brown (13) and
nut brown (11): 50gm of
each. 3/3/3/4 4½cm toggles
for front; 2 3cm toggles for
motif on back.

Needles
One pair of 6mm needles.

Tension
Using 6mm needles and
measured over st st, 14 sts
and 20 rows = 10cm
square.

A chunky-weight duffle coat that is suitable
for all the family. It is worked using the
intarsia method (*see* Techniques, page 8).

Back
Using 6mm needles and red, cast on 52/57/
61/94 sts. Work in k2, p2 rib for 2½cm, then

The graph opposite
should be followed for
the back of the adult's
coat. The crosses indicate
where the toggles and
toggle cords should be
fixed, and the dotted line
indicates the line of chain
stitch, which should be
embroidered in light
brown.

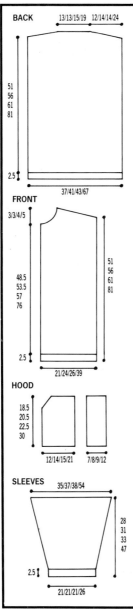

BACK

13/13/15/19 12/14/14/24

51
56
61
81

2.5

37/41/43/67

FRONT

3/3/4/5

48.5
53.5
57
76

51
56
61
81

2.5

21/24/26/39

HOOD

18.5
20.5
22.5
30

12/14/15/21   7/8/9/12

SLEEVES

35/37/38/54

28
31
33
47

2.5

21/21/21/26

cont in st st starting with a k row for 10/16/24/12 rows. Working the small graph for the first three sizes and the large graph for the fourth size, place as follows: k3/6/8/8 sts. Work first row of appropriate graph, k to end. Next row: p3/5/7/7 sts. Work second row of graph, cont in st st, working graph as placed until it is complete. Cont straight in base colour only until work measures 51/56/61/81cm, ending with a WS row. Cast off 8/9/10/11 sts at beg of the next 2 rows. Cast off 9/10/10/11 sts at beg of the next 2 rows. **Large size only:** cast off 11 sts at beg of the next 2 rows. **All sizes:** cast off remaining 18/19/21/28 sts.

Left front

Cast on 30/33/36/54 sts in red and work in k2, p2 rib for 2½cm. Now cont in st st with front edge border as follows:
RS rows: knit to last st, k1, k1b.
WS rows: sl 1, k2, purl to end.

This will give a neat front edge to jacket. Rep these 2 rows until work measures 48½/53½/57/76cm, ending at front edge.
Shape neck: cast off 7/7/7/12 sts at beg of the next row, work to end, work 1 row, now dec 1 st at neck edge on every row until 17/19/20/33 sts remain. Cont in st st until work measures same as back to shoulder, ending with RS of work facing. **Shape shoulder:** cast off 8/9/10/11 sts at beg of the next row, work 1 row, cast off 9/10/10/11 sts at beg of the next row. **Adult size only:** work 1 row, cast off remaining sts.

Right front

Work as for left front, reversing all shapings and making sure that the front border edge is kept correct.

Sleeves

Cast on 30/30/30/36 sts in red and work in k2, p2 rib for 2½cm. Now work in st st, inc 1 st at each end of every following 5th/5th/5th/4th rows until there are 50/52/54/76 sts. Cont in st st until work measures 28/31/33/47cm. Cast off all sts.

Patch pockets (Make 2)
Cast on 14/16/18/20 sts in red and work in st st for 10/11/12/15cm. Now work in k2, p2 rib for 2½cm. Cast off ribwise.

Hood (Side sections: work 2)
Cast on 17/20/21/30 sts in red and work in st st until work measures 13½/15½/17½/23cm, ending at front edge.
Next row: knit.
Next row: sl 1, p 2 sts together, p to end.
Rep these 2 rows until 13/15/17/24 sts remain, then cont in st st until work measures 18½/20½/22½/30cm. Cast off all sts.

Centre back section
Cast on 10/11/12/16 sts in red and work in st st until back section fits neatly along shaped edge of side section. Cast off all sts. Sew centre back section to shaped edges of side sections to form hood.

Edging
Using red and with RS of work facing, pick up and knit approximately 72/82/102/120 sts evenly around front of hood. Work in k2, p2 rib for 2½cm. Cast off ribwise.

Toggle holders
Cast on 6/6/6/8 sts in red and work in st st, dec 1 st at beg of every row (dec inside edge stitch to give a neat edge) until 2 sts remain. Work 1 row, then work remaining 2 sts tog and fasten off. Work a further 5/5/5/7 toggle holders to match.

Toggle cords
Cast on 2 sts in red. Work in st st to make a cord 8cm long, fasten off (make 3/3/3/4 in total). Using blue wool, cast on 2 sts. Work in st st to make a cord 4cm long, cast off (make 2/2/2/2 in total). Using red wool, make a single chain 6cm long (make 3/3/3/4 in total).

Label
Cast on 2 sts. K 1 row, inc 1 st at each end of

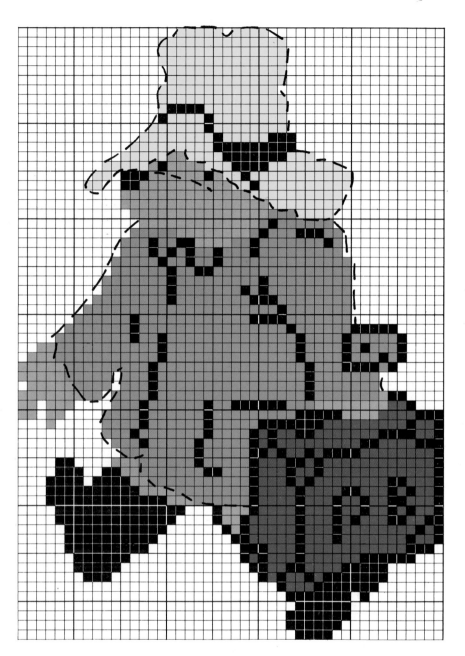

Incorporate this graph into the child's duffle coat. Outline the hat, coat and snout in chain stitch, following the dotted lines, using yellow for the hat, blue for the coat and light brown for the snout.

the next row, the 3 following alt rows and the 3 following rows (14 sts). Work straight for 29 rows. Next row (WS): knit. Cast off. Using black wool, embroider 'Please look after this bear. Thank you', as shown on the diagram.

Making up
Join shoulder seam. Set in sleeves, sew into place. Sew pockets into position on fronts setting at top of rib in the position desired. Join side and sleeve seams using a flat seam.

Pin toggle holders into position with the long edge facing the inner bands. Sew side edges into place. Fold red toggle cords in half, tuck into holders and stitch down firmly. Tie narrow toggle cord around toggle and sew ends into opposite holders. Sew blue toggle cords onto Paddington's coat, secure toggles to other side with a double strand of wool. Using chain st, outline the hat and coat on smaller sizes (*see* Techniques, page 12) as indicated on the small graph.

HUG ME DRESS

A huge "huggable" fluffy teddy dress with dolman sleeves. Easy to knit, it is worked in one piece using the intarsia method (*see* Techniques, page 8).

Dress

Using 5½mm needles and peacock, cast on 64 sts. Work in k1, p1 rib for 22cm, inc 8 sts evenly across the last row of rib (72 sts).

Change to 6mm needles and, starting with a knit row, commence following graph in st st, inc 1 st at each end of every alt row until you have 170 sts. Cont following graph without shaping for another 24 rows.
Shape neck: next row (RS): k63, leave remaining sts on a spare needle and work on this first set of sts only, p 1 row. Dec 1 st at neck edge on next row and the next 2 alt

Materials
Wendy Soft Touch – peacock (58): 550gm; rose (59), yellow (55), white (54) and black (65): less than 50gm of each. 2 googly eyes 2½cm in diameter.

Needles
One pair of 5½mm and one pair of 6mm needles.

Tension
Using 6mm needles and measured over st st, 16 sts and 18 rows = 10cm square.

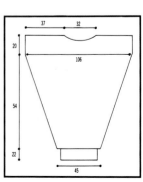

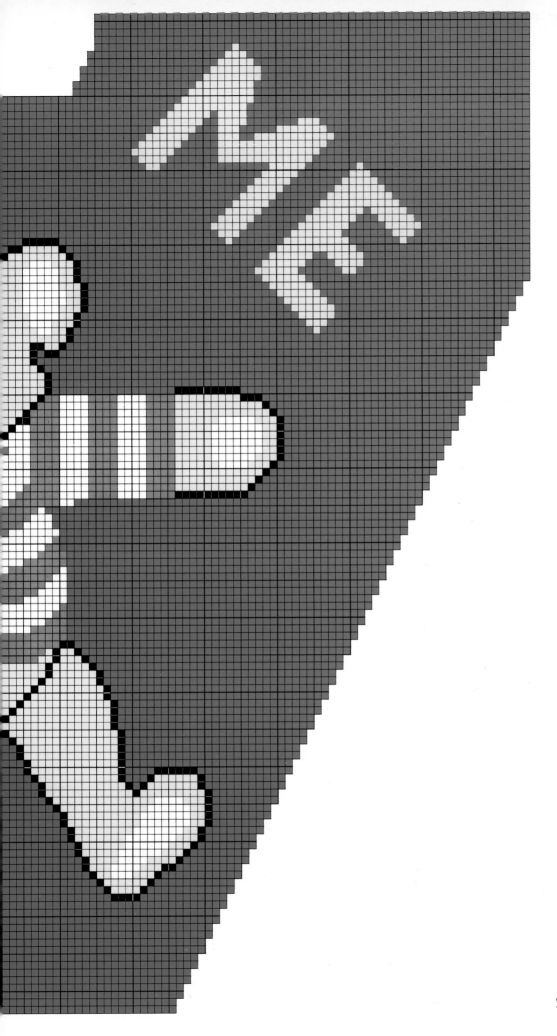

Follow this graph to complete the front of the sweater. The black dotted line indicates where teddy's mouth should be embroidered in running stitch; the red dotted line indicates the fold; and the crosses indicate where you should attach teddy's eyes.

rows, work 4 rows without shaping, then inc 1 st at neck edge on next row and the next 3 alt rows. Leave sts on a spare needle and rejoin yarn to centre front. Cast off 44 sts, k to end. P 1 row. Dec 1 st at neck edge on next row and the 3 following alt rows. Work 4 rows. Inc 1 st at neck edge on next row and the next 3 alt rows. P across the 63 sts. Cast on 44 sts for centre back. P across the 63 sts held for other side of neck. Cont in base colour only, work 24 rows without shaping, then dec 1 st at each end of the next row and every alt row until you have 72 sts. Change to 5½mm needles and work in k1, p1 rib for 22cm. Cast off loosely.

Collar

Using 6mm needles, cast on 100 sts. Work in k1, p1 rib for 22cm. Cast off very loosely.

Cuffs

Using 5½mm needles, cast on 36 sts. Work in k1, p1 rib for 4 rows, then cont in rib, inc 1 st at each end of every alt row until you have 72 sts. Cast off.

Making up

Join side seams and cuff seams using a flat seam. Join the short ends of the collar with an invisible seam. Stitch cuffs into place (with the wide end against the sleeve). Sew collar around the neck, keeping the seam at the centre back of jumper. Embroider mouth using running stitch. Attach eyes.

BIG BEAR

A classic bear made using the traditional toymaking techniques. Big Bear is approximately 58cm high when seated.

Instructions

All the pieces are worked using st st throughout, the knit side being the right side of your work. Each piece should be knitted separately and shaped by increasing and decreasing as indicated on each individual graph. Shapings should always be made on the second stitch and the stitch before the last stitch of every row and not on the very edge of the pieces. To increase, simply knit in the front and back of the stitch and to decrease, knit or purl two together according to whether you are working on the right side or wrong side of your work. Always work in the direction indicated by the arrow. To save confusion, label each piece as it is completed with the correct part name.

Work graphs as follows:

Head side: knit 2 pieces (one reversed).
Body back: knit 2 pieces (one reversed).

Materials

Wendy Soft Touch – sable (62): 600gm. Wendy Aran – antelope (516): 50gm. Scraps of black wool. 1½kgm of terylene stuffing. One pair amber glass eyes; one plastic nose.

Needles

One pair of 5mm needles.

Tension

Using 5mm needles and measured over st st, 18 sts and 24 rows = 10cm square.

The graphs on this page
and on pages 79, 80 and
81 should be worked
separately. The letter A
indicates that you should
use a lighter shade of
brown for these pieces;
the letter B indicates that
a darker shade should be
used to complete the foot
pads and paw pads.

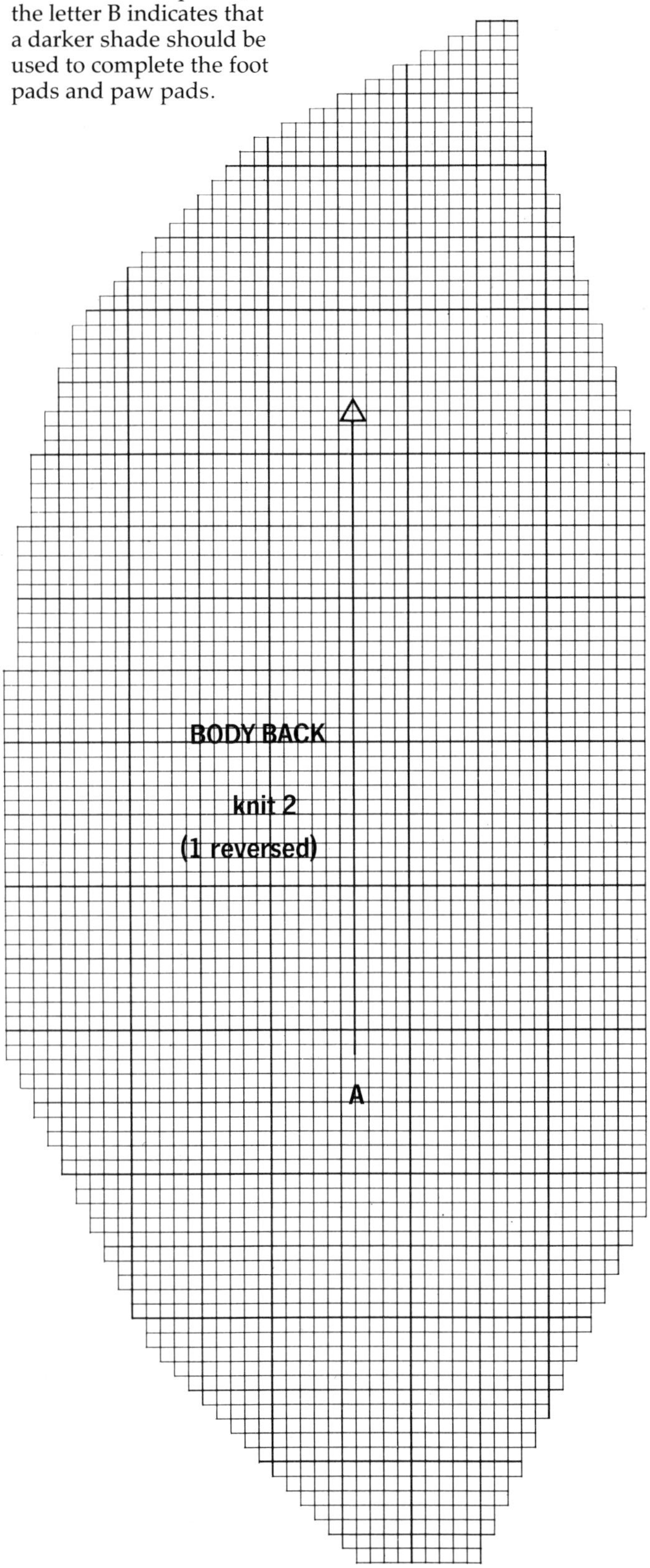

BODY BACK

knit 2
(1 reversed)

A

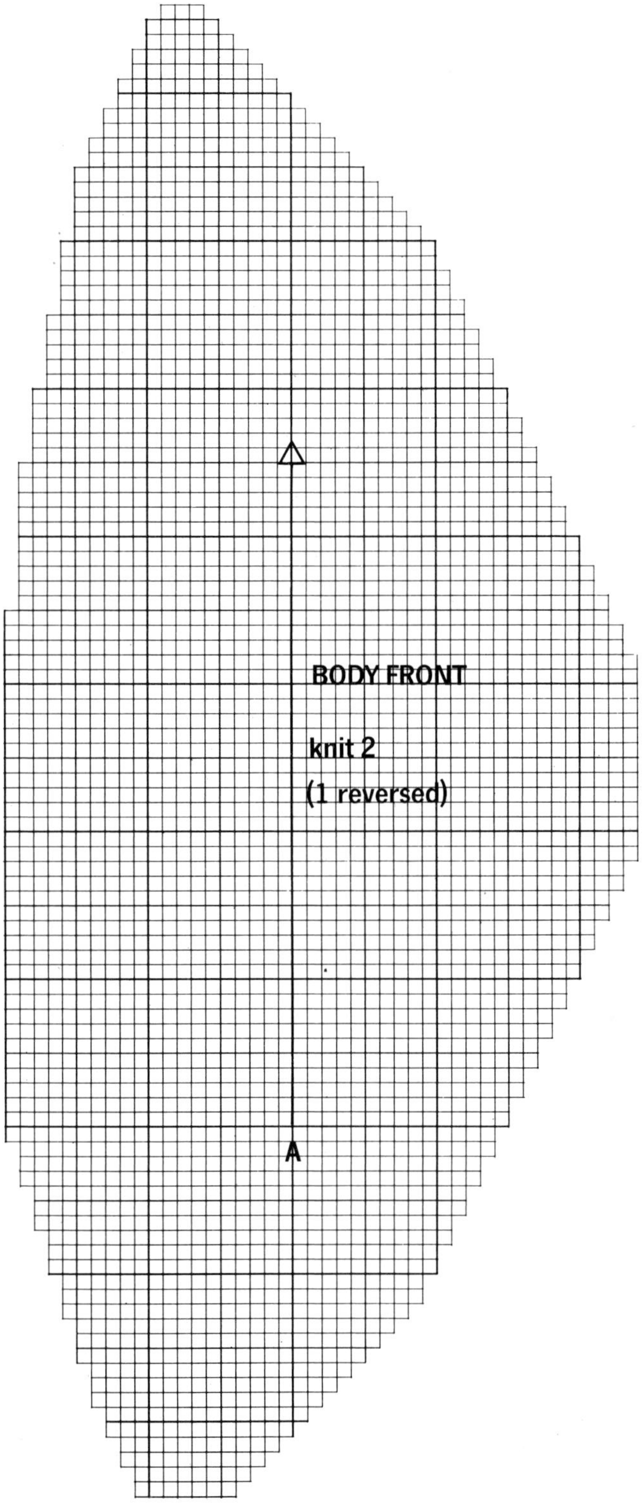

BODY FRONT

knit 2
(1 reversed)

A

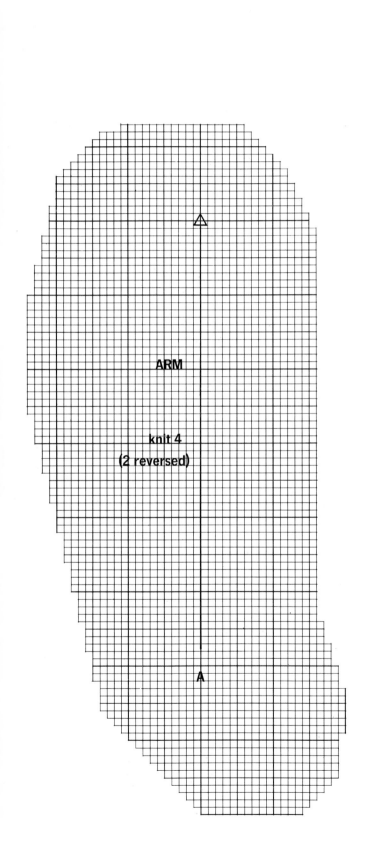

ARM

knit 4
(2 reversed)

A

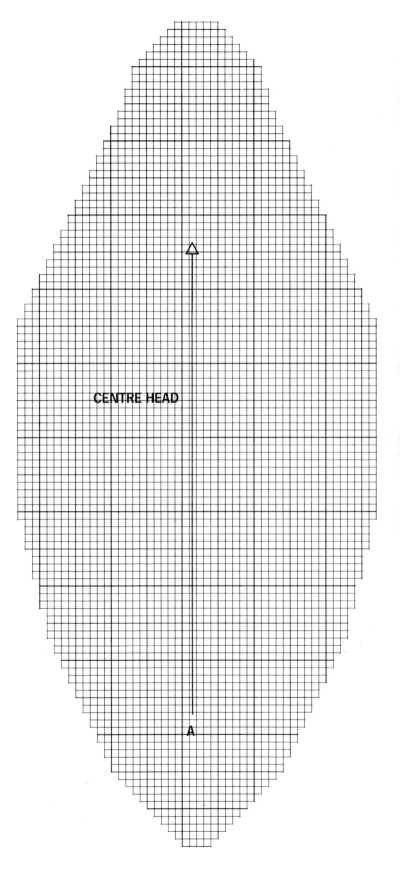

CENTRE HEAD

A

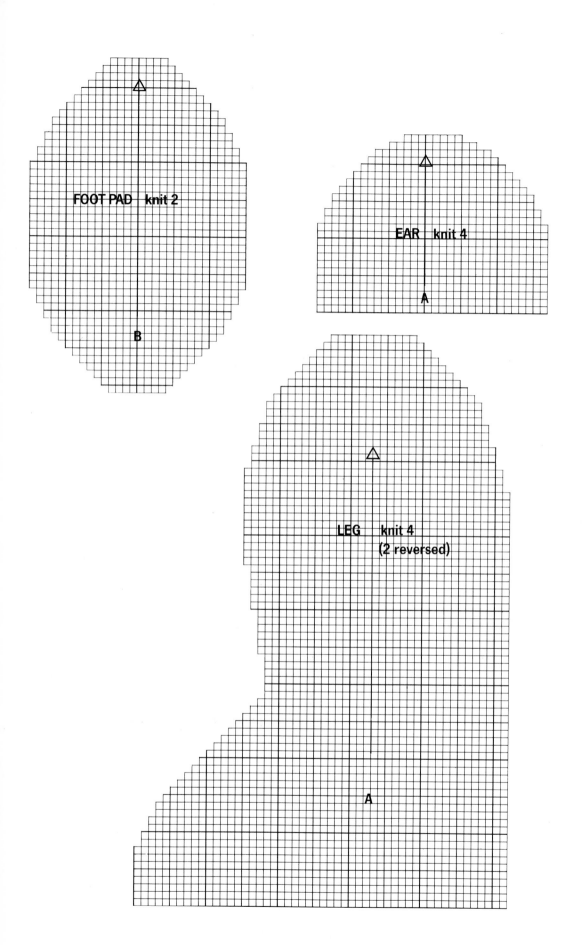

FOOT PAD   knit 2

B

EAR   knit 4

A

PAW PAD   knit 2

B

LEG   knit 4
(2 reversed)

A

80

Body front: knit 2 pieces (one reversed).
Arm: knit 4 pieces (2 reversed).
Leg: knit 4 pieces (2 reversed).
Centre head: knit 1 piece.
Ear: knit 4 pieces.
Paw pad: knit 2 in brown.
Foot pad: knit 2 in brown.

Making up
All seams should be narrow and oversewn.

Arms
Sew the paw pads curve to curve about
2½cm in from the bottom of the inner arms.
With RS together, sew the inner armpiece to
the outer armpiece leaving the shoulder end
open and stuff firmly.

Legs
With RS of work together, stitch up the side
seams of the outer and inner legs, leaving an
opening at the top for stuffing and an
opening at the bottom for the footpads.
Stitch the footpads into position. Stuff the
legs firmly, adding extra stuffing to thigh
areas.

Body
Sew each front piece to back piece. This will
form seams that run up the bear's sides.
Now carefully stitch the two halves of the
body together forming seams that run up
teddy's tummy and back, leaving an opening
at the back for stuffing. Stuff firmly and sew
up opening.

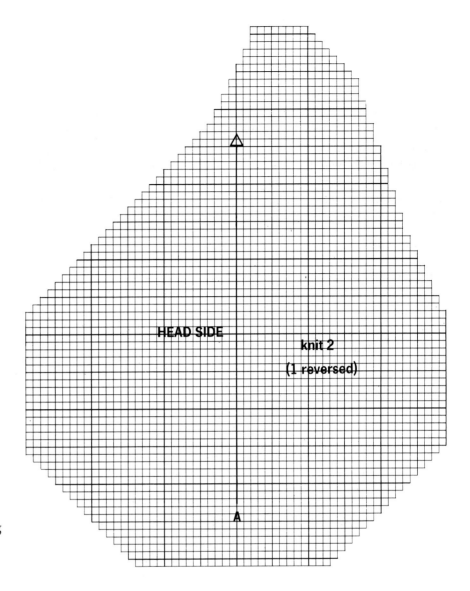

HEAD SIDE

knit 2

(1 reversed)

A

Head
Take the two head sides and, with RS
together, sew up from the neck opening to
the top of the snout. Then sew on the head
centre, starting from the back of the neck
opening and stitching right around to the
nose and back down the other side to the
neck opening. Turn work right side out and
stuff. Attach nose to top point of snout and
embroider on mouth using one vertical and
one horizontal stitch. Place eyes in position
(to the desired expression) and fix firmly.
Place head on top of body and tack into
position, adding extra stuffing to keep neck
firm. Tack arm-tops and leg-tops to body,
placing them in a sitting position and
stuffing firmly as you go. Using mohair,
oversew all pieces into position as tacked,
working twice round each piece to ensure
they are secure.

Ears
Place two earpieces RS together and sew
around curved edge. Turn RS out and, using
a small backstitch, sew a line about 1cm in
from the curve to form a ridge at the top.
Sew bottom edge together, gathering slightly
as you go. Pin into position using the
photograph as reference and sew firmly into
position. Rep for other ear.

KIDS' SQUEAKY JUMPERS

Materials
Wendy Family Choice DK
wool – chilled cream or
valentine: 250/300/300/
350gm; blue (216) and
yellow (267): 50gm of
each. A scrap of black
yarn. A small amount of
terylene wadding. One
flat plastic squeaker.

Needles
One pair of 3¼mm and
one pair of 4mm needles.

Tension
Using 4mm needles and
measured over st st, 24 sts
and 32 rows = 10cm
square.

A bright jumper decorated with an appliqué
teddy that squeaks. You can personalize this
jumper by Swiss darning a child's name

using our lettering chart. Knitted in stocking
stitch, the jumper will fit children aged 2–3,
3–4, 5–6 and 7–8 years.

Personalize the jumper
by using Swiss darning
(*see* page 13) to embroider
a child's name on it.
Select the appropriate
letters from the graph
opposite.

Front

** Using 3¼mm needles, cast on 76/84/88/96 sts.

Row 1: k1, *k2, p2, rep from * to last 3 sts, k3.

Row 2: k1, *p2, k2, rep from * to last 3 sts, p2, k1.

Rep these last 2 rows until work measures 5cm, ending with a first row. Inc 3/1/3/1 sts evenly across next row (78/85/91/97 sts). Change to 4mm needles.** Work in st st for 94/100/116/130 rows. **Shape neck:** next row: k28/31/34/36, turn. Cont on this set of sts as follows: dec 1 st at beg of the next row.*** Dec 1 st at neck edge on the next and every following alt row until 24/26/29/31 sts remain. Work 5/5/7/7 rows without shaping, finishing on a WS row.

Shape shoulder: cast off remaining sts.*** With RS of work facing, rejoin yarn to remaining 48/51/55/58 sts. Next row: k17/17/19/19 sts. Slip these sts onto a stitch holder. K to end. Cont working on the last 31/34/36/39 sts as follows: dec 1 st at the end of the next row. Work from *** to ***.

Back

Work as for front from ** to **. Cont working in st st until back measures the same as front to shoulder, finishing on a WS row. **Shape shoulders:** next row: cast off 24/26/29/31 sts. K31/33/33/35 sts. Cast off remaining 24/26/29/31 sts. Slip centre 31/33/33/35 sts onto a stitch holder. Break off yarn.

Sleeves (Both alike)

Using 3¼mm needles, cast on 40/44/44/44 sts. Work 5cm in rib as for front, finishing on a WS row.

Change to 4mm needles and work in st st, inc 1 st at each end of the next and every following second row for the first three sizes (fourth row for the fourth size), until you have 50/50/50/92 sts, then on every following 4th/4th/4th/6th row until you have 78/84/90/96 sts. Cont straight until sleeve measures 29/33/37/43cm (including rib), finishing on a WS row. Cast off loosely. Join left shoulder seam.

Neckband

With RS of work facing and using 3¼mm needles, k31/33/33/35 sts from back neck stitch holder. Pick up and k16/17/18/19 sts down left side of neck. K17/17/19/19 sts from front neck stitch holder and pick up 16/17/18/19 sts up RS of neck (80/84/88/92 sts). Beg

with a second row, work in rib as for front for 8 rows. K 1 row. Work 10 more rows in rib, cast off loosely in rib. Join right shoulder seam, join neckband seam and sl st cast-off edge of neckband to pick-up edge.

Making up

Join sleeves to jumper using a narrow backstitch. Join sleeve and side seams using flat seams throughout.

Inside pocket

Using 4mm needles and base colour, cast on 20 sts. Work in st st until work measures 8cm. Cast off.

MOTIFS

Teddy

Beginning with the legs, using 3¼mm needles and yellow yarn used double, cast on 6 sts. K 4 rows. Cast off 3 sts at beg of the next row. Inc 1 st at each end of the next row

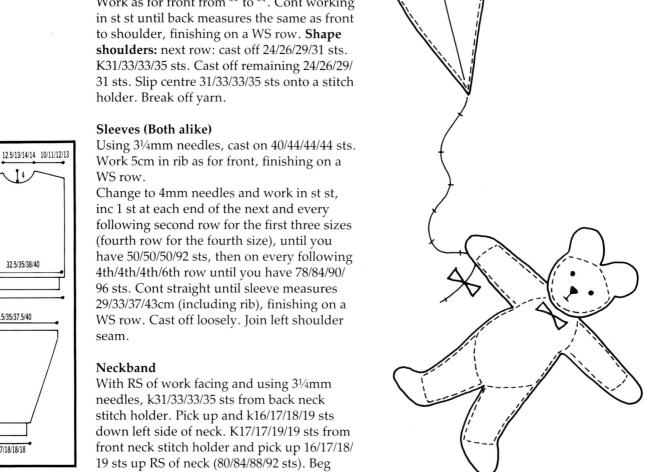

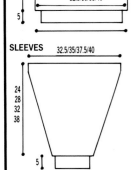

(5 sts). K 7 rows. Break off yarn, slip these sts onto a spare needle. Work second leg as for first, but end up working 6 rows instead of 7. Knit across the 10 sts from both legs, k 10 rows. Cast on 8 sts at beg of the next 2 rows, k 4 rows, dec 1 st at each end of the next row. Cast off 9 sts at the beg of the following 2 rows (6 sts). K 1 row. Inc 1 st at each end of the next row (8 sts). K 9 rows. Inc 1 st at each end of the next row (10 sts). **Shape ears** next row: k5, turn, k3, k2 tog, turn, k2 tog. K2, turn, cast off 3 sts. Fasten off. Rejoin yarn at inner edge k3, k2 tog, turn, k2 tog, k2, turn. Cast off 3 sts. Fasten off.

Kite
Using 3¼mm needles and red, cast on 2 sts. K 1 row, inc 1 st at each end of the next row, the following 4th row and the 4 following 5th rows. K 1 row, dec 1 st at each end of the next row and the 4 following alt rows (4 sts).

Next row: k2 tog, knit last 2 sts together, fasten off.

Small bow (Make 2)
Using 3¼mm needles and blue wool used double, cast on 4 sts. K 3 rows, k2 tog, k2 tog, k 2 rows, inc 1 st at each end of the next row, k 2 rows, cast off.

Bow-tie

Using 3¼mm needles and blue wool used double, cast on 10 sts. K 3 rows, dec 1 st at each end of the next row, the following 4th row and the following alt row, k 10 rows. Inc 1 st at each end of the next row, the following alt row and the following 4th row. K 3 rows, cast off.

Sewing on the motifs
Pin the teddy motif on the front of the jumper, placing it at an angle on the bottom corner. Leaving ears, paws and feet free, stitch as illustrated on the diagram and stuff the legs, arms, head and tummy. Wind blue yarn several times around the centre of a small bow and stitch below teddy's chin. Sew kite into position in the opposite top corner. With black wool, make one horizontal stitch across the kite and one stitch from top to bottom. Arrange a curling trail of black wool from the kite to teddy's paw and catch into position. Sew a small bow just before end of trail. Embroider teddy's face as positioned on diagram.

Bow-tie: fold the bow-tie in half, RS together, and join just before the increasing starts. Stitch bow to centre front neck just below the neck rib. Using red wool, make small knots on the bow for spots.

Inside pocket: position pocket so that the bottom edge is level with the bottom of teddy's tummy. Using running stitch, join to inside of jumper leaving a top opening and insert plastic squeaker.

N.B. Remember to remove the squeaker before washing the jumper.

TEDDY BASEBALL JACKET

A sporty jacket worked in an aran-weight yarn using the intarsia method (*see* Techniques, page 8).

Left front
** Using 3¾mm needles and yellow, cast on 51 sts.

Materials
Wendy Action Knit – green (514): 500gm; yellow (539): 150gm; red (527): 50gm; black (530): 50gm; white (510) and blue (513): less than 50gm of each. Ascot DK wool used double – amber (412): less than 50gm. 8 buttons, 1cm in diameter.

Needles
One pair of 3¾mm and one pair of 4½mm needles.

Tension
Using 4½mm needles and measured over st st, 19 sts and 24 rows = 10cm square.

The graph overleaf should be followed to complete the back of the jacket (*see* page 90). The graph on page 90 should be incorporated into the left front.

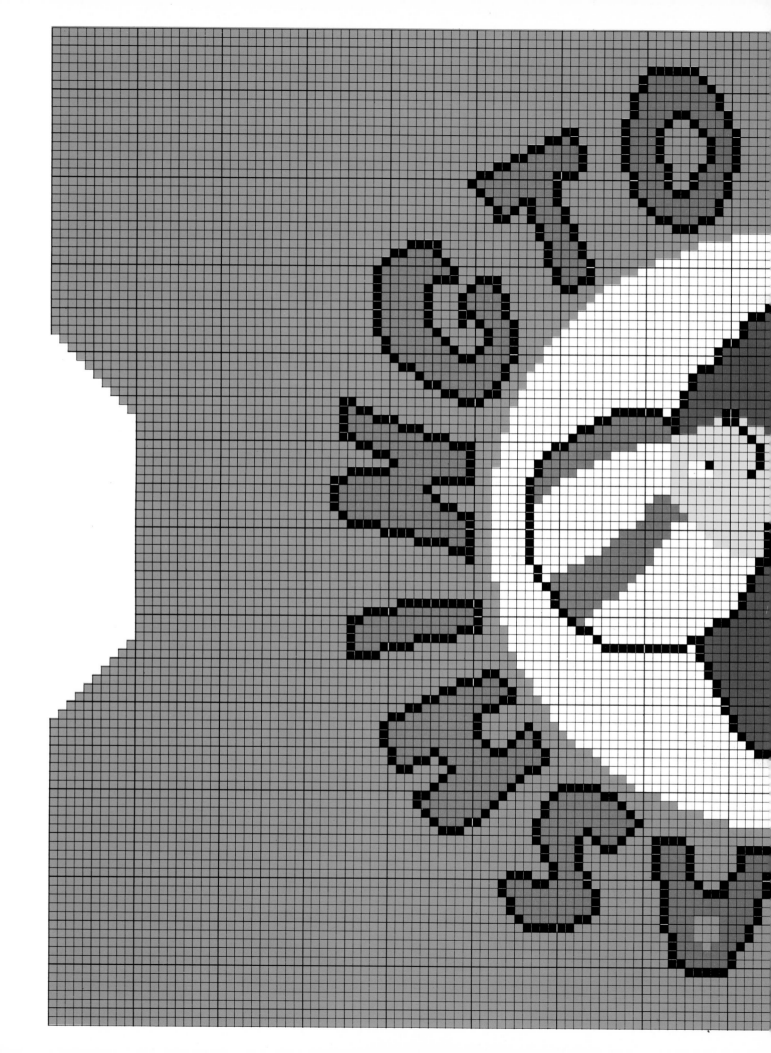

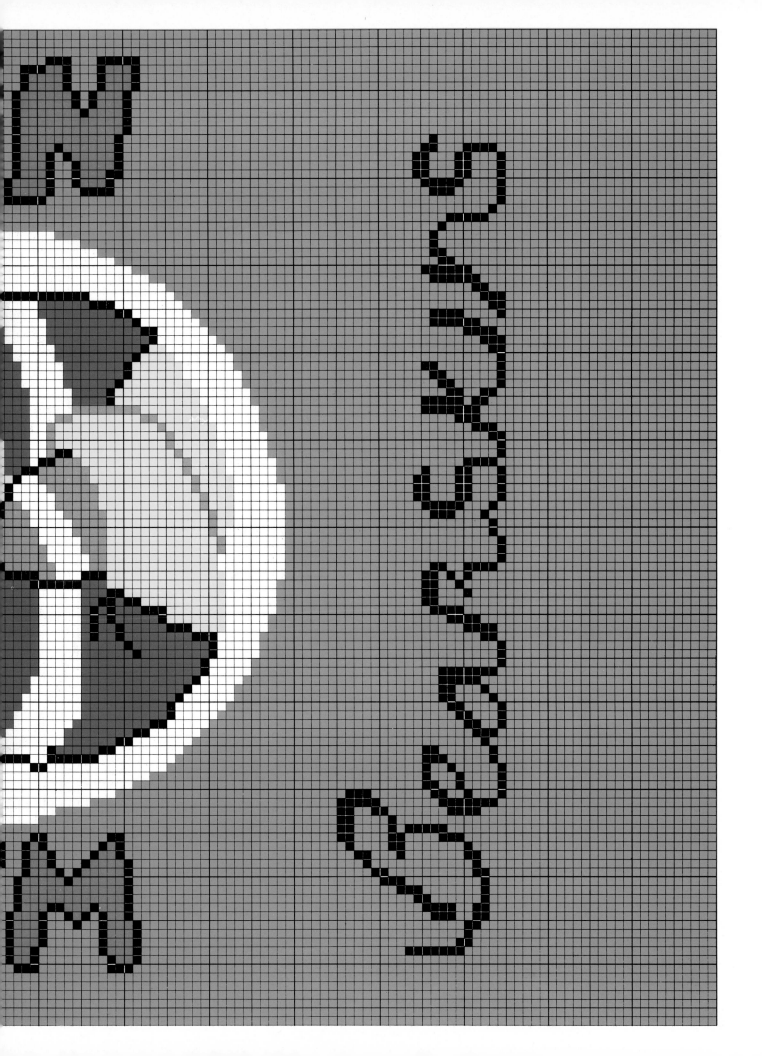

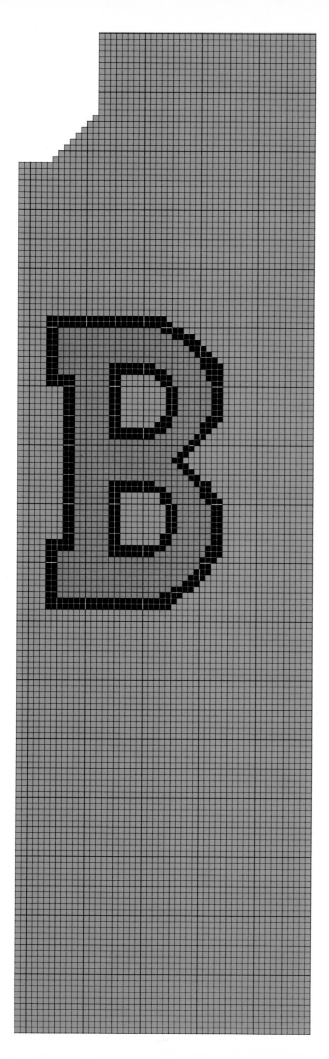

Row 1: k1, *p1, k1, rep from * to end.
Row 2: p1, *k1, p1, rep from * to end.
Row 3: work as for row 1.
Row 4: using green, purl.
Rows 5–8: using green, rep rows 1 and 2 twice.
Row 9: using yellow, knit.
Row 10: using yellow, work as for row 2.
Rows 11 and 12: using yellow, rep rows 1 and 2 once.
Row 13: using green, knit.
Row 14: using green, work as for row 2.
Rows 15–20: using green, rep rows 1 and 2 three times.
Row 21: using green, work as row 1.
Row 22: work as row 2 but inc into last stitch (52 sts).
Change to 4½mm needles and commence following the graph, working in st st to neck shaping: next row: cast off 6 sts, p to end. Dec 1 st at neck edge on every row until 38 sts remain. Work a further 14 rows in st st, cast off.

Right front
Work as for left front, but reverse shapings and ignore motif.

Back
Using 3¾mm needles and yellow, cast on 107 sts. Work the 21 rows of rib as for front.
Row 22: inc 7 sts evenly across row (114 sts).
Change to 4½mm needles and commence working in st st, following graph to neck shaping.
Shape neck: work 44 sts, slip remaining sts onto a spare needle and, working on this side only, dec 1 st at neck edge on every row for 9 rows. Work 1 row, cast off. Rejoin yarn to remaining sts. Cast off centre 26 sts, work to end. Rep shaping as for other side of neck, cast off.

Sleeves (Both alike)
Using 3¾mm needles and yellow, cast on 43 sts. Work the 21 rows of rib as for front and inc 12 sts evenly across the 22nd row (55 sts).
Change to 4½mm needles and commence following the sleeve graph, working in st st.

Pocket linings (Make 2)
Using 4½mm needles and green, cast on 33 sts. Work 17½cm in st st, finishing on a WS row. Cast off.
Join shoulder seams.

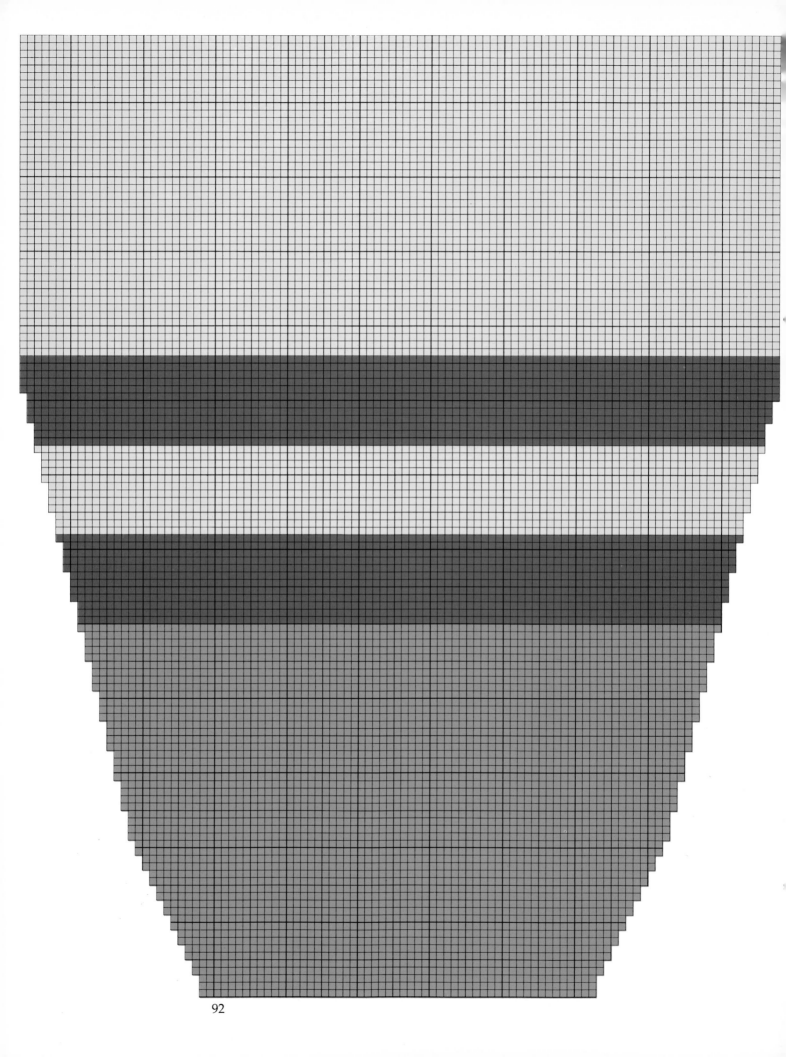

Follow the graph opposite to complete both sleeves.

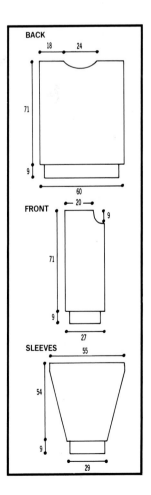

BACK
18   24
71
9
60

FRONT
20
9
71
9
27

SLEEVES   55
54
9
29

Neckband

Using 3¾mm needles, green and with RS facing, pick up and k 22 sts up right front neck, 8 sts down right back neck, 26 sts across back neck, 8 sts up left back neck and 23 sts down left front neck (87 sts).

Row 1: p1, *k1, p1, rep from * to end.
Row 2: k1, *p1, k1, rep from * to end.
Row 3: work as for row 1.
Row 4: using yellow, knit.
Rows 5 and 6: using yellow, rep rows 1 and 2.
Row 7: using green, purl.
Row 8: using green, work as for row 2.
Rows 9 and 10: using green, rep rows 1 and 2.
Row 11: using green, rep row 1.
Row 12: using yellow, knit.
Rows 13 and 14: using yellow, rep rows 1 and 2.
Row 15: using green, purl.

Using green only and commencing on a second row, work a further 14 rows in rib. Cast off in rib. Fold neckband in half onto the wrong side and sl st into position.

Buttonband

Using 3¾mm needles, green, and with RS facing, starting at the top of the neckband, pick up and k 145 sts evenly down left front to lower edge. Work the first 13 rows of rib as given for neckband. Using yellow, cast off in rib.

Buttonhole band

Using 3¾mm needles, green, and with RS facing, starting at the lower edge, pick up and k 145 sts evenly up right front to top of neckband. Work the first 7 rows of rib as given for neckband. Next row (make buttonholes): rib 5, *yrn, dec 1 st, rib 17, rep from * to last 7 sts, yrn, dec 1 st, rib to end. Commencing on the 9th row, work a further 5 rows in rib as given for neckband. Using yellow, cast off in rib. For a man's jacket, reverse the positions of the button and buttonhole bands.

Making up

Join side seams with a narrow backstitch, leaving 17½cm open above the rib for the pocket linings.

Pocket edgings

Using 3¾mm needles, green and with RS facing, pick up and k 39 sts evenly along open edge of front side seam. Work the first 13 rows of rib as given for neckband. Using yellow, cast off in rib. Join the edge of the pocket linings to the back side seam with an invisible seam. Sl st pocket linings to fronts to make pocket. Sew sleeves into position and join sleeve seams.
Sew on buttons.

STOCKIST INFORMATION

All the sample garments illustrated in this book were knitted in Wendy yarns. For information on your local stockist write to:

Wendy
Carter & Parker Ltd
Gordon Mills
Guiseley
West Yorkshire LS20 9PD

As many of the designs contain small quantities of several different colours, Melinda Coss offers individual kits containing only the quantities of Wendy yarn necessary to complete each garment. In addition, buttons, embroidery threads and trimmings are included where appropriate. Contact Melinda Coss at 1 Copenhagen Street, London N1 0JB (telephone 01-833 3929). The kits are available by mail order only.

For those who wish to substitute different yarns, weights are given throughout to the nearest 50gm ball. To obtain the best results, you must ensure that the tension recommended on your selected yarn matches the tension printed in our pattern. We cannot guarantee your results if this rule is not followed.

For teddy accessories (eyes, noses, stuffing and so on) write to:

Pick 'n Choose
Dept P.N.
56 Station Road
Northwich
Cheshire CW9 5RB